THE HISTORY OF
KAMBUJA-DESA

THE HISTORY OF Kambuja-Desa MODERN CAMBODIA

R.C. MAJUMDAR

MANOHAR
2026

First published 1943
Reprinted 2024, 2025, 2026

ISBN 978-93-6080-701-6 (hardbound)
ISBN 978-93-6080-222-6 (ebook)

Published by
Ajay Kumar Jain *for*
Manohar Publishers & Distributors
4753/23 Ansari Road, Daryaganj
New Delhi 110 002

Printed and bound in India

PREFACE

In July 1942 I was invited by the university of Madras to deliver a course of lectures under the Sir William Meyer (Endowment) Lectureship, 1942-43. These lectures are published here in the form in which I delivered them, early in March 1943, with the addition of the footnotes and a list of Inscriptions, on which the study of the subject is primarily based. The scope and object of these lectures have been sufficiently indicated at the beginning of Lecture I, and I shall consider my labours amply rewarded if they serve to awaken an interest in, and promote the study of a highly important but little-known subject. The series of works on ancient Indian colonisation in the Far East which I planned nearly twenty years ago have not yet been completed. Three volumes dealing with Champā (Annam) and Suvarṇadvīpa (Malayasia) are out, and the remaining two volumes dealing with Kambuja (Cambodia), Burma and Siam still await publication. These two volumes will deal more comprehensively with the subject covered by these lectures. In view of the present situation in the country, it is difficult to say when, if ever, those two volumes will see the light of the day. Till then, the present work may be regarded as completing the series of my studies on the history of ancient Indian colonies in the Far East.

As inscriptions have been frequently referred to in the course of these lectures, I have added at the end a list of old Kambuja inscriptions, arranged chronologically as far as possible. The serial number is quoted in the text against each inscription to enable the reader to find out the necessary details by a reference to the list. In some cases a short summary is given of the contents of the Inscription in order to draw the attention of the reader either to its general importance or to certain special features to which it has not been possible to refer in the body of these lectures. The list is not, of course, exhaustive, the total number of Kambuja inscriptions, so far discovered, amounting to nearly 900. And it is needless to add that most of the inscriptions contain a great deal more than it has been possible to indicate in the short summaries of contents.

In conclusion I take this opportunity to thank most sincerely the Syndicate of the University of Madras for having invited me to deliver these lectures —an invitation, which I consider to be a high distinction and a great privilege. I would also like to offer cordial thanks to my esteemed friend Prof. K. A. Nilakanta Sastri M.A., who presided over these lectures, and whose company and hospitality I enjoyed in ample measure during my stay at Madras.

4 Bepin Pal Road
Kalighat, Calcutta,
May 8, 1943.

R. C. Majumdar.

ABBREVIATIONS.

1. Aymonier=Le Cambodge by E. Aymonier, 3 Vols. Paris, 1900-1903.
2. BCAI.=Bulletin de la Commission Archeologique de l'Indo-chine.
3. BEFEO=Bulletin de l'Ecole Française d'Extrême-Orient.
4. Champa=Ancient Indian Colonies in the Far East, Vol. I, Champā by Dr. R. C. Majumdar, (Lahore, 1927).
5. Chatterji=Indian Influence in Cambodia (Calcutta University, 1928).
6. Corpus=Inscriptions Sanscrites du Cambodge by M. Barth and A. Bergaigne (Paris, 1885).
7. Et. As.=Etudes Asiatiques (Hanoi, 1925).
8. Ferrand-Textes=Relations de voyages et Textes Geographiques Arabs, Persans at Turks relatifs a l'Extrème Orient by G. Ferrand (Paris, 1913-14).
9. Inscriptions=Inscriptions du Cambodge by G. Coedès (Hanoi, 1937).
10. Maspero=L'Empire Khmer by G. Maspero (Phnom Penh, 1904).
11. Suvarnadvīpa=Ancient Indian Colonies in the Far East, Vol. II, Suvarnadvīpa, (Part I, Political History, Part II, Cultural History) by Dr. R. C. Majumdar (Dacca, 1937).

CONTENTS

Lecture I

THE BEGINNINGS OF INDIAN COLONISATION IN CAMBODIA.

I propose to review, in a course of six lectures, the history of the Indian colony of Kambuja-*deśa*[1] (modern Cambodia) and some aspects of the civilisation that the Hindus, using this term in its broadest sense, had introduced in this distant land. I shall try to describe how the small isolated Hindu kingdoms in different parts of Cambodia were welded into a mighty kingdom that stretched from the Bay of Bengal to the sea of China, how the essential spirit of Hindu culture was transplanted to this distant corner of Asia, how the Hindu religion inspired it to build monuments whose massive grandeur still excites the wonder of the world and far surpasses anything known so far in India, how art and institutions, created on Indian models, grew and developed a unique character, how this mighty colonial kingdom flourished for more than a thousand years fed by constant streams of civilisation flowing from the motherland, and at last met with inevitable decline when this perennial source itself decayed and ceased to flow. The treatment of the subject will necessarily be of a general character, as minute discussions of controversial points will be out of place in a public lecture. But I shall try to bring together the most reliable data available on the subject, and when these series of lectures will be published in the form of a book, add notes to explain the different view-points and the source and authority of my statements. Two considerations have induced me to follow this method. In the first place I wish to awaken the general interest in a subject which is at present but little known. For although the history of Greater India constitutes an important and brilliant chapter of the History of India, it has not yet appealed to the general public, and even to professed students of Indian history to any considerable extent. Secondly, I wish to emphasise the broad features of the history and civilisation of Kambuja in order that a solid foundation may be

1. The term Kambuja-deśa, or simply Kambuja has been used to indicate the ancient Hindu colonial kingdom, in the modern French Protectorate of Cambodia

laid for further detailed studies on the subject. It may be noted that there is at present no text which gives a critical review of the history of Kambuja as a whole, in the light of modern researches on the subject.[2] It is necessary for a comprehensive study of the subject to prepare a skeleton to which flesh and bone may be added later. The absence of such a skeleton hampers the efforts to study the subject in detail by utilising the abundant data pouring in every year from the archaeological researches of the French savants. Such a study will be facilitated by the establishment of a solid framework which it will be my endeavour to reconstruct in course of these lectures.

Although the history of Hindu colonisation in Cambodia is the principal subject of this course of lectures, it is necessary, in order to view it in its true perspective, to make a broad survey of the state of Indo-China at the moment when the Hindus first came into contact with it. This is particularly important, for, as we shall see later, the Kambuja empire in its greatest extent embraced nearly the whole of this region with the exception of Upper Burma and Tonkin. The Hindu culture and colonisation in this vast region must be viewed on the background of the land and the peoples in

2. The following texts deal with the general history of Kambuja.

1. M. Aymonier—*Le Cambodge*, 3 Vols. The main work is devoted to a description of the different localities in Siam and Cambodia with notices of the monuments and inscriptions. The concluding volume, published in 1904, gives a brief outline of the political history.
2. G. Maspero—*L'Empire Khmer* (1904). This is the first systematic treatment of the political history of Kambuja. But it is only a very brief sketch, the ancient period being comprised in 27 pages.
3. A. Leclere—*Histoire du Cambodge*—A comprehensive history of the country from the earliest to modern times. (1914).
4. Etienne Aymonier—*Histoire de l'ancien Cambodge* (1918). It is a popular treatment of the subject, and was originally published in a Paris newspaper. It gives no authority for the statements made.
5. Dr. B. R. Chatterji—*Indian Cultural Influence in Cambodia* (1928). The only scholarly work, in English, on the subject. It treats the political history and different aspects of culture of Kambuja.

It will be seen that none of the texts is later than 1928, the year memorable for the new theory of P. Stern about the evolution of the art of Kambuja, which has practically revolutionised our conception of the history and progress of Kambuja culture. A number of new inscriptions discovered since 1928 have also profoundly modified our views about the political history of Kambuja.

and amid which they flourished. We would, therefore, begin with a short account of these two, emphasising particularly those features which throw light on, or help the study of, subsequent history.

The great Indo-Chinese Peninsula covers the whole of the main-land of Asia to the east of India and south of China. Shut off by the high chains of hills from the continent on the north, it has easy means of communication, by sea and land, with both India and China. Large and broad at the north it gradually narrows as it advances to the south, ending in a long strip of land known as the Malay Peninsula. In addition to this, it covers the region now known as Burma, Siam, Laos, Cambodia, Tonkin, Annam and Cochin-China. The last four form a French Protectorate, while Laos is divided between this Government and Siam.

The region, distinctly marked off from the rest of Asia, has no physical unity like its neighbour, India or China. Situated between two oceanic systems, the Bay of Bengal and the China Sea, it has a large coast-line with numerous harbours facilitating contact between one another and with the outside world. The interior is, however, mostly difficult of access, being intersected by long spurs of hills into a number of small plateaus and valleys without easy means of inter-communication. The most characteristic physical feature of the Peninsula is a series of parallel ranges of hills running generally north to south throwing spurs in all directions, with a large river, also running north to south, enclosed between each pair of hills forming so many water-sheds. On the extreme east and west we have two great ranges running along the whole coast line and separated from the sea by a narrow strip of plains. One starting from the south of China constitutes the Annamite Hills, and the other from Assam and Manipur passes through Arakan, Tenasserim and Malay Peninsula. The other parallel ranges form the water-sheds between the rivers Irawaddy (with its branch Chindwin), the Sittang and the Salween in Burma, the Mekong and the Menam in the Central region, and the Red River in Tonkin. These rivers, carrying silt from the uplands, formed the deltas which constituted rich alluvial fertile plains of smaller or bigger size, according to varied physical conditions of the country. These deltas on the sea-coast formed a striking contrast to the hills and dales of the interior, and formed, along with the narrow strips of land in Annam and Malay Peninsula between the hill-range and the sea, the strong centres of Hindu colonisation in the Peninsula. With the exception of Upper Burma which had direct access from India by land, these deltas formed the main strongholds of Hindu culture, and the bases from which it radiated, principally along the river valleys, towards the interior. It is, therefore, not a mere accident that the most important Hindu colonial kingdoms were founded, and the Hindu culture and civilisation exercised an abiding influence, mainly in these regions, whereas the Hindu influence in the interior was comparatively slow, less profound and of shorter duration.

The people who inhabited the Indo-Chinese Peninsula at the time when the Hindus first came into contact with it belonged to different races and spoke a number of tongues. Without attempting to be too precise and scientific from ethnological and linguistic points of view, which would require a separate treatment with lengthy elaboration of details, beyond the scope of the present review, I may refer to some of the main classifications which are generally agreed to by the scholars.

First we come across two groups of people, known as Tibeto-Burmans and Mon-Khmers, who are generally believed to have migrated from India in pre-historic times, and in any case certainly show greatest resemblance in physical features and linguistic forms with some non-Aryan tribes in India still living in hilly regions remote from centres of civilisation. The Tibeto-Burmans consisted of a large number of Mongoloid tribes, and those who peopled Upper Burma show the greatest resemblance to the Abor and Mishmi tribes in Eastern India.

The designation Mon-Khmer, applied to a group of peoples, is derived from the names of its two principal tribes viz., the Mons and the Khmers. Their languages belong to the same family as those of the Munda and Khasi tribes in India, and the Semang and Sakai of the Malay Peninsula. The name Austro-Asiatic is now applied to this group of languages, and it is believed that the tribes speaking them, at least the Mons and Khmers, originally lived in India, and came to Indo-China when they were pressed by invading Aryans. The Mons settled in Lower Burma and proceeded thence, along the valley of the Menam, to the interior of Siam proper. The Khmers peopled Cambodia and moving towards the west met their kinsmen, the Mons, in Siam. Their mutual relations would be referred to later.

Two other important groups were the Chams, who lived in what is now called Annam, but was known formerly as Champā, and the Malays who settled in the Peninsula, now known after them. These two belonged to the large group which constitutes today the predominant element of the population in Sumatra, Java,

Bali and other islands of the Indian Archipelago or Indonesia. It was recognised long ago that the languages of the Chams and Malays belong to the same family as that of Polynesia, and the name Malayo-Polynesian was at first applied to this group. Since then, however, Melanesian, Polynesian, Micronesian and Indonesian (or Malay) languages have all been proved to belong to the same family to which the new name Austronesian has been applied.

So far we are on sure grounds. But there is a theory which, though not generally accepted, cannot be omitted in the present review, as it concerns the general question of Indian colonisation in the Far East, and puts its history in an altogether different light. The great German scholar Schmidt who first established the existence of the linguistic family called Austro-Asiatic, referred to above, has proposed further to connect with it also the Austronesian and establish a larger linguistic unity which he calls Austric. He also indicates the possibility of an ethnic unity among the peoples whose linguistic unity is thus assumed. In other words, Schmidt regards the peoples of Indo-China and Indonesia such as the Mons, Khmers, Chams and the Malays as belonging to the same race as the Munda and allied tribes of Central India and the Khasis of North-eastern India. He regards India as the original home of all these peoples who, starting from India towards the east, at first spread themselves over the whole length of the Indo-Chinese Peninsula and then over all the islands of the Pacific Ocean up to its eastern extremity. This theory, we must remember, has not yet found general acceptance among scholars, but we must not lose sight of the possibility that the Aryanised India, in establishing colonies in the Far East, was merely repeating or continuing the work which had been inaugurated long long ago by many other peoples inhabiting the same land before the advent of the Aryans.[3]

While the coastal regions of Indo-China were thus peopled by races whose language bears a strong affinity with that of non-Aryan peoples of India, and all or most of whom had probably migrated from India in pre-historic ages, the interior of the Indo-Chinese Peninsula was dominated, at the beginning of the Christian Era, by groups of peoples who belonged to the Thai race.[4] This race is now well-known from its most important settlement in Siam, which has recently changed its name to Thailand. The Siamese have put a

3. This topic has been fully treated in my work '*Suvarnadvīpa*', Part I, pp. 11 ff.

4. For an account of the Thais cf. *T'oung Pao*, 1897, p. 53; 1909, p. 495.

new interpretation on the word Thai, meaning free, an invention designed to emphasise the liberation of their country from the yoke of Kambuja in the thirteenth century A.D. The Thailand, however, etymologically means, not the "Land of the Free" as the Siamese would have us believe, but the land of the Thai tribe. For this name Thai has been regularly used, centuries before the independence of Siam, by various other branches of the tribe who had numerous settlements in the uplands of Indo-China. As the Thais are so far little known in this country, but intimately bound up with the history of Kambuja and the expansion of Hindu culture in Indo-China, I shall set forth briefly their origin, and later discuss their history, so far as it has been ascertained on reliable evidence.

The Thais are a Mongolian tribe and are generally believed to be ethnically related to the Chinese. In any case, they, or at least a large group or groups of them, lived in southern and south-eastern part of the country now known as China. About three centuries before the Christian era, or probably somewhat earlier, the Thais in large groups migrated to the south and south-west. Two of their early settlements were in the regions which we call today Tonkin and Yunnan. During the early centuries of the Christian era a steady stream of the Thais proceeded towards the west and south-west and set up numerous other principalities. The dates and gradual stages of their advance cannot be fixed with certainty, but by the 8th or 9th century A.D. they had advanced as far as the Upper Irawaddy and Salween rivers in the west, and the frontiers of Siam and Cambodia in the south.

Thus when the Hindu colonists first came into contact with Indo-China, about the beginning of the Christian Era, or probably somewhat earlier, they found there peoples of diverse races in the primitive state of civilisation. Everything indicates that the Hindus came by land-routes to upper Burma but, for the rest, they mainly followed the sea-route. For we find that the Mons, the Khmers, the Malays and the Chams were profoundly influenced by these colonists and strong Hinduised kingdoms were founded in their lands all along the sea-coast. Thus, beginning from the west, we find the Hinduised Mon kingdoms of Dhanyavatī, Basim, Rāmāvati, Haṁsāvatī and Suvarṇabhūmi (or Sudhammavati) on the western and southern coasts of Lower Burma corresponding respectively to Arakan, Bassein, Rangoon, Pegu and Thaton. Further south, beyond Dvāravatī in Siam and a number of small kingdoms in the Malay Peninsula were the Hinduised Khmer kingdom of Kambuja in Cambodia and Cham kingdom of Champā in Southern Annam. All these kingdoms bore a strong impress of Hinduism in all aspects of their culture and civilisation. Thus excepting Tonkin, which came early under the Chinese influence, the rest of the coastal regions, and particularly the delta of the Irawaddy, Salween, Menam and Mekong rivers were seats of powerful Hindu kingdoms.

As regards the interior of Indo-China, the Indian colonists seem to have settled in large number in Upper Burma, and the Hinduised Tibeto-Burmans founded important principalities there. This region came early under the influence of Indian culture which has still a complete hold of the people. From eleventh century onwards the Hinduised Tibeto-Burmans established their political authority over the Hinduised Mon kingdoms of the coastal regions of Burma, and ultimately the two peoples and cultures were fused together, though the Mons, or Talaings, the name by which they are better known, still form a distinct element in south-eastern parts of the land. The Hinduised Mons, before they were merged into the Tibeto-Burmans, spread their cultural influence along the coast of Bay of Bengal throughout the Tenasserim region, and down the valley of the Menam river and its tributaries up to the very heart of modern Siam. There they met with the Hinduised Khmers who had established their influence in the lower valley of the Menam. The contact between the Hinduised Mons and Khmers. and the gradual expansion of the latter towards the north at the expense of the Mons and the Thais will be described in course of the discussion on Kambuja.

The Thais, as already noted, peopled nearly the whole of the uplands of Indo-China to the east of Burma and north of Siam and Cambodia. The region was full of mountain ranges and dense forests, interspersed with valleys, and the rivers which flowed through them were not navigable on account of torrents and rapids. The history of Indian colonisation in this region and the extent to which it was influenced by the Hindu culture and civilisation are but imperfectly known to us, and this is partly due to the comparative inaccessibility of a large part of this region to modern explorers. But although we are not in a position to give a detailed and systematic account of the Hindu colonisation in this area, some broad facts may be stated indicating its general nature and extent.

The two most important Thai principalities in Indo China were those in Yunnan and Tonkin. These were the farthest from India and nearest to China. It should be remembered that about the time when the Thais first settled in these regions the Chinese kingdom proper did not extend beyond the Yang-se-kiang river, but its rulers tried to extend their political authority over the Thais, whom they called barbarians, living in the south and south-west. It is unnecessary for our present purpose to describe the long-drawn struggle between the two, and it will suffice to say that the Thais in Yunnan, though occasionally defeated and subjugated for longer or shorter periods, never ceased to defy the authority of the Chinese, and ultimately established their independence. By the seventh century A.D. they had freed themselves completely from Chinese control, and established a powerful kingdom which played an important rôle in the history of Indo-China for more than six hundred years. The kingdom is generally, though not very correctly, designated as Nan-chao, but it is called Videha-rājya, and its capital is named Mithilā, in the native chronicles. The history of Tonkin was more chequered. There the Annamites were subjugated to China for a long period, and it was not until the tenth century A.D. that they regained their independence and set up a very powerful kingdom which comprised not only Tonkin, but also the northern part of modern Annam. The Annamites undoubtedly formed a branch of the Thais though some are of opinion that they had a strong admixture of the Mon blood.[5] The Annamites are designated as Yavanas in native chronicles, and adopted Buddhism.

The effective political authority exercised by the Chinese over Tonkin for more than a thousand years resulted in the introduction of Chinese culture in Tonkin, and this is the only region in Indo-China whose civilisation may be said to have been definitely moulded by that people. Far different was the case with Yunnan. Although ethnically allied to the Chinese and living immediately on its border, the Thais in Yunnan seem to have been brought under the cultural influence of India, either directly by the Indian colonists or indirectly through the Hinduised states in Burma. In the absence of epigraphic records and other contemporary evidence it is difficult to give a precise or detailed account, but broad general indications are not wanting. The great French scholar Pelliot has brought together a number of isolated facts and traditions which

5. *BEFEO*. XXI. pp. 260 ff., 274-75.

seem to prove that the Hindu culture, which has left such a strong impress upon Upper Burma, also made its influence felt in Yunnan. Although it is generally believed, on the authority of Chavannes, that the Thais of Nan-chao were ignorant of writing, Pelliot has drawn attention to one or two inscriptions in unknown characters, which probably originated in Nan-chao. These characters appear to be of Hindu origin. It is characteristic of the Hinduised people of Indo-China, that they sought to create a new India by giving well-known Indian place-names to their towns and kingdoms. According to this practice we find the name Gandhāra applied to a part of Yunnan. A part of it, as noted above, was also called Videha-rājya and its capital was named Mithilā, the kingdom being sometimes referred to as Mithilā-rāṣṭra. Local traditions affirm that Avalokiteśvara came from India and converted the region to Buddhism. It is said that when, towards the close of the 8th century A.D., the ruler of this kingdom became enamoured of Chinese civilisation, seven religious teachers of India rebuked the king. In the first half of the ninth century A.D. a Hindu monk named Chandragupta, born in Magadha and therefore designated Māgadha, led a brilliant career of a thaumaturgist in Yunnan. There was in Yunnan the famous Pippala cave, the Bodhi tree, the sacred hill Gṛdhrakūta and many other localities associated with Buddhism. A Chinese traveller of the tenth century A.D. refers to a local tradition that Śākyamuni obtained the Bodhi near Lake Ta-li in Yunnan. The Buddhist influence in Yunnan is still attested by two bells of the 11th century with inscriptions in Chinese and Sanskrit. The king of Nan-chao had the title Mahārāja and also another Hindu title, which means the king of the east. According to local tradition the royal family was descended from the great Asoka. Rasiduddin, writing in the 13th century, not only calls the country Gandhāra but asserts that its people originated from India and China. All these demonstrate that the Thais of Yunnan had imbibed Hindu culture and civilisation to a very large extent.[6]

There were many other Thai States to the west and south of Yunnan. The Chinese refer to the Brāhmana kingdom of Ta-tsin to the east of the mountain ranges that border Manipur and Assam, and another about 150 miles further east, beyond the Chindwin river. Whether these were mainly peopled by Hinduised Thai we

6. For Nan-chao cf. the detailed account of Pelliot in *BEFEO* IV, pp. 152 ff, where other references are given.

cannot say. But a group of Thai states, united in a sort of loose federation, which occupied the region between the Irawaddy and the Salween, was known as Kosāmbi. The southern part of this is now known as the Shan States, the Shan tribe being that branch of the Thais which proceeded farthest in the western direction. To the east of these were a series of small states extending from the frontier of Yunnan to those of Kambuja and Siam. These were, from north to South, Ālavirāṣṭra, Khmerarāṣṭra, Suvarṇagrāma, Unmārgaśilā, Yonakarāṣṭra, Haripuñjaya and many others, whose internecine wars, and consequent changes in boundaries and sometimes also in names, are recorded in the local chronicles, written in Pali, of which we possess quite a large number. These Pali chronicles give detailed accounts of the ruling dynasties and the religious foundations of the different local states. These cannot be regarded as historical annals in the sense in which we understand the term, but they leave no doubt that the mainspring of the civilisation of most of the Thai States lay in India and not in China. The evidence of the Pali chronicles is fully corroborated by the archaeological finds, for images of the Gupta style and those of somewhat later date have been found in these regions. It is a significant fact that these Thais, though ethnically belonging to the same race as the Chinese, and living nearer to them, should have been brought so profoundly under the influence of Hindu culture and civilisation rather than Chinese.[7]

There is no need to feel surprised about the Indian influence in these regions of Indo-China. For we have definite evidence that as early as the second century B.C. there was regular communication, by overland route, between East India and Yunnan. In the second century B.C. Chang-Kien, the famous Chinese ambassador in Bactria, was surprised to find there Chinese silk and bamboo products which, he learnt on enquiry, came from Yunnan and Sez-Chuan across the whole breadth of Northern India right up to Afghanistan and Bactria beyond the Hindukush. The two Indian Buddhist missionaries who visited China in the first century A.D. most probably passed through the upper valley of the Irawaddy and Yunnan. There are references also to the regular communication between China and Western Asia, via Yunnan, Upper Burma and India in the second and third centuries A.D. I-tsing also refers

7. For an account of the Thai States in central Indo-China cf. *Et, As.* Vol. II, pp. 98 ff.

to 20 Chinese pilgrims as having gone to India through Yunnan and upper Burma. The geographical memoir of Kia Tan, written between 785 and 805 A.D., describes two routes leading from Tonkin through Yunnan and Burma to India. That this route was well frequented in the tenth century A.D. is attested by the fact that the 300 religious missionaries sent by the Chinese Emperor to India in 964 A.D. in search of sacred texts returned by way of Yunnan.[8] The large scale raids of the Manipuris in Burma and of the Burmese in Manipur prove the use of these routes down to the middle of the eighteenth century A.D. Thus although the direct land-route from India to hinterland in Indo-China was comparatively little known and less used in very recent times, the case was different in ancient and medieval periods, and a constant stream of Indian emigrants passed through this route to spread Indian culture and civilisation in this region.

Having thus made a broad survey of Indo-China we may now proceed to a more detailed discussion of Kambujadeśa which forms the subject-matter of this course of lectures. This kingdom varied in its boundaries at different periods of its history and covered, at its greatest extent, the territories which correspond to Siam, Cambodia, Laos and Cochin-China and comprised the valleys of the Mekong and the Menam. The Kambujadeśa proper corresponds to Cambodia and Cochin-China, comprising the lower valley of the Mekong river, south of the island of Khong and the range of hills known as Dangrek mountains.

The valley of the Mekong comprises the whole of modern Cambodia with the exception of the three provinces of Kampot on the west and Svay Rieng and Thbong Khmum on the east. The last two are, however, watered by the two branches of the river Vaicos, which are joined to the Mekong across the vast marshy plains by innumerable canals, both natural and artificial, and may be regarded as its tributaries forming a common Delta in Indo-China.

It has been suggested that the name of the river Me-kong is derived from Mā-Gaṅgā, the mother Ganges.[9] Whatever we may

8. For an elaborate discussion of these routes with full reference to authorities cf. *BEFEO*. IV. pp. 131 ff.

9. The name Mekong or Mekhong is believed to be composed of two words, indigenous *me* meaning chief or mother, and *kong*, derived from Sanskrit Gaṅgā. It would thus be equivalent to mother Ganges. (Leclere-*Cambodge*—p. 2. f.n.i).

think of this, there is no doubt that this river played as important a rôle in the history of Kambuja as the Ganges did in the early history and civilisation of Northern India.

The Mekong is to Cambodia what the Nile is to Egypt. It is its very life. Its banks supply the habitations of the people and its regular annual inundations fertilise the country. The region beyond the reach of the flood-water is almost an arid desert.

From the point, below the rapid of Prah Patang, where the Mekong enters Cambodia, it is enlarged, and its bed is nearly doubled, by the large marshy depressions running parallel to its course, which have been mostly formed by the old beds of the river. It covers the country by its ramifications and is joined, near Phnom Penh, to the vast lake of Tonle Sap, about 60 miles to the north-west, by a wide sheet of water, full of islands. From this point of junction the river branches off into two wide streams, connected by numerous cross canals forming islands in the intervening region, till they both fall into the China Sea forming the rich delta of Cochin-China.

When in June the sun rays melt the snow on the Tibetan plateau and the waters come rushing down the hill streams, the Mekong and its tributaries rapidly rise, cut through their steep banks by numerous sluices and overflow the whole region right up to the borders of the forest on the 'Highlands'. Then behind the steep river banks, marked by fruit trees, gardens and dwelling houses, one sees only a vast sheet of water submerging beneath it the lakes, the marshes and the plain. It is not till October that water recedes and the ground becomes dry enough for cultivation.

The vast area of Lowlands', annually inundated by the Mekong, forms practically the whole of the inhabited area of Cambodia at the present day. In the region north of Phnom Penh, the people are settled mostly in groups along the bank of the Mekong and its tributaries, or on the borders of the Highlands. In the dry season they even temporarily settle in the outlying area for purposes of cultivation, but immediately after the harvest is over, they return to their homes on the river in time before it is flooded again.

In the region south of Phnom Penh the habited area is not so strictly confined to the river-banks. There the people also spread here and there, wherever there are high lands fit for cultivation. This region abounds in palm-trees, and viewed from the top of a high temple looks like a vast palm-forest dotted by marshes or rice fields.

In this region of annual inundation called 'Lowlands', the discovery of archaeological ruins proves that the modern settlements closely correspond to those of old times. Only it appears that in the northern part, the modern inhabited area has extended a little beyond the old, whereas the case is just the reverse in the south (e.g. the province of Ba Phnom).

It will be shown later that it was precisely in the 'Lowlands', and rather to its southern part, that we can trace the earliest habitation and political and cultural development in Cambodia. Obviously, the earliest Hindu colonists chose the region where conditions of livelihood were the easiest. The large number of simple brick monuments found in this region were probably constructed by the first settlers before the sixth century A.D. In that case we must hold that the lower valley of the Prek Tonot, the districts of Bati and Prei Krebas and part of the district of Treang must have been densely peopled in old days, for the remains of the brick temples are particularly numerous in this area. Most of the modern temples cover the sites of these ancient ones and many of the mounds, covered with vegetation, which emerge above the rice fields in the valley of the Prek Tenot hide the ruins of these ancient temples.

The region to the north and west of the 'Lowlands', beyond the reach of the flood, may be termed the 'Highlands', although its mean height is not very much above the sea-level. It extends up to the Dangrek mountains in the north and the hill-ranges of Phnom Kravanh and Sang Re to the west. The low grounds of this region are full of muddy depressions covered with high thick grass, while the higher part is an arid limitless forest. The tropical dense forest of tall beautiful trees, with a rich and varied flora and bushy soil, is few and far between. The greater part of it is covered by a reddish gravel stone, without moss and almost bereft of grass, interspersed with vast areas covered with naked sandstone, offering for days a monotonous sight to the eyes of the wearied traveller. The rivers in this area are dry for the greater part of the year and are full to the brim in the rainy season.

The whole of this region now lies deserted and uncultivated. One may travel for days together without coming across the least sign of human beings. Only the deers, buffaloes and wild elephants roam undisturbed across these arid fields. A few miserable hamlets may be seen here and there at the foot of the hills near the springs where the descendants of the primitive wild tribes still maintain a precarious existence. Otherwise death-like solitude reigns supreme where once stabely buildings stood and a mighty empire and civilisation grew. For it is this area which comprises in its southern part the whole of the Angkor region where the Hinduised Kambuja civilisation reached its high-water mark of development and reared magnificent temples and big populous cities with strongly fortified walls and gates, grand palaces, tanks, parks, and secular structures of all kinds. Human effort and ingenuity, after a hard struggle with nature, converted this region into a flourishing centre of civilisation, by building roads, canals, tanks, bridges and dams. So long as the streams of Hindu colonists continued to flow and infused vigour and energy into the populace, this region continued to flourish. But as soon as they were dried up, the people reverted to their old lethargy. Nature triumphed, and once more the region relapsed to its old primaeval condition. But still the handiwork of man did not altogether perish. Gigantic temples and ruins of mighty cities and palaces have survived the destructive forces of nature and still tell the tale of a bygone age to awestruck travellers in this wild forest.

So far about the land. We may now pass on to its inhabitants. The earliest people who are known to have inhabited the region we have just described were the ancestors of the Khmers who still form the predominant element of the people of Cambodia. The modern name Khmer was used in ancient times also both by the people themselves as well as by the foreigners, along with the name of Kambuja, of whose origin we shall speak later. The name Khmer appears as Kvir and Kmir in the old inscriptions of Champā (Annam) and as Comar in the writings of the Arabs. The use of this name Comar by the Arabs has been a source of considerable confusion, as early writers have identified it sometimes with Cape Comorin and sometimes with Kāmarūpa (Assam). Its identity with Khmer country or Cambodia is now well established.[10]

It is very likely that the country was originally inhabited by savage hill tribes whom the Khmers conquered and forced to take shelter in hills and jungles. Of this there is no definite evidence. But to the north of Cambodia, beyond the Dangrek mountain, lived the Laotians after whom the country is still called Laos. They belonged to the Lao race and were mostly savage hill tribes, and still retain most of their primitive characteristics. Their settlements

10. Sometimes the Arab writers themselves seem to confuse Kāmarūpa with Comar.

extended up to the outer fringe of the Hindu colonies but they generally kept aloof and though influenced by the Hindu colonists never attained to any high degree of culture and civilisation.

As already noted above, the Mons, who inhabited the lower valleys of the Irawaddy and the Salween in Burma, extended further south, and formed along with the Laos and Khmers the primitive population of modern Siam. Throughout the course of history a distinction is noticeable between this heterogeneous Mon-Khmer people of Siam and the pure Khmers of Cambodia. The Mon-Khmers were intolerant of the political suzerainty of the Khmers and always regarded themselves as a rival power.

The Khmers and Mons thus constituted the principal elements of population in the country which constituted the Hindu kingdom of Kambuja. At the time the Hindu colonists first settled there these people were in an almost semi-savage condition. According to the Chinese accounts the people, both men and women, went about naked, and decorated themselves with tattoo marks. The Chinese expressly state that it was the first Indian ruler who made the women wear clothes.

What attracted the Indians first towards Cambodia it is difficult to say. Perhaps it was merely a stage in the course of extensive colonial enterprises which marked the Indians during the early centuries of the Christian Era. The general question of the Indian colonisation in the Far East has been discussed by me elsewhere[11] and need not be repeated here. It will suffice to say that trade, missionary spirit and military adventures all contributed towards it, and the Indians advanced towards Indo-China both by sea and land-routes. Reference has been made above to the establishment of Indian colonies not only in Upper Burma but also in the hilly regions in the upper valleys of the Irawaddy, the Salween and the Mekong rivers, and we have seen how the Indians advanced further south along these rivers and established colonies and states in the hinter-zone of Indo-China. Whether they advanced in this way as far as Cambodia proper along the banks of either the Menam or the Mekong rivers, we cannot definitely say. But we may recall in this connection a passage in Hiuen Tsang's Travels the full significance of which is not often realised. After finishing the description of Samatata which corresponds roughly to Southern and

11. *Champa*—Introduction.

Eastern Bengal the pilgrim remarks: "Going north-east from this to the borders of the ocean we come to the kingdom of Shi-li-cha-ta-lo (Śrīkshetra)", and he names in succession five other kingdoms which were not visited by him, but of which he gained information at Samataṭa. All these kingdoms have not been satisfactorily identified, but two of them I-shang-na-pu-lo or Īśānapura and Mo–ha-chan-po or Mahāchampā undoubtedly correspond to Cambodia and Annam.[12] It is a legitimate inference from the statement of Hiuen Tsang, and particularly the context in which it is made, that there was a regular intercourse by land between E. India and these remote regions before the seventh century A.D. The reference to Īśānapura, is specially significant, for the Kambuja king Īśānavarman, after whom it was named, ruled in the second and third decades of the seventh century A.D., and was thus almost a contemporary of Hiuen Tsang. That his name was known in E. India before 638 A.D. when the Chinese pilgrim visited it, certainly shows that Indians had a fairly regular communication with Cambodia. The intercourse between Cambodia and Burma is also referred to in the early annals. Recent political events have reawakened our interest in the Burma-India land route, but, as already noted above, it seems to have been fairly well-known and regularly used more than a thousand years ago. The Burmese annals prove that throughout the medieval period Burma had regular intercourse through land with E. India on the one hand and Siam, Cambodia and Annam on the other. There is thus no inherent difficulty in presuming a connection between E. India and Cambodia by overland route. Indeed one scholar seems to have been so much convinced of the facility of this route that he seriously suggested that the Kambuja dynasty which temporarily occupied Northern and Western Bengal in the tenth century A.D. came from Cambodia.[13]

Whatever we may think of a possible land-route to Cambodia, there can be no doubt that there was communication by sea from very early times. The Periplus of the Erythræan Sea proves that at least as early as the first century A.D., ships from Indian ports regularly sailed to Malay Peninsula, and there are indications that the sea-route to China *via* Straits of Malacca was also in use.

12. Beal, II, 199-200; Watters, II, 187-189. For the identifications cf. *JRAS*. 1929 pp. 1,447. Hindusthan Review, July, 1924.
IHQ. II, p. 250; IV, p. 169; *Ind. Ant.* LVIII, p. 57; LV; p. 113.
13. Chatterji, p. 279.

Ptolemy's accounts indicate further progress of this maritime intercourse as he refers to various Indian place-names in Indo-China, Malay Peninsula and the islands of the Indian archipelago. One of the Chinese chronicles, the History of the Liang dynasty, compiled during the first half of the seventh century A.D., explicitly refers to Indian ambassadors coming by the Southern Sea to China during the period 147-167 A.D.[14] As the vessels in those days kept close to the coast as far as possible, Southern Cambodia must have furnished one or more important halting stations in the distant voyage between India and China. We must, therefore, presume that the Indian mariners possessed a knowledge of Cambodia at the beginning of the Christian era, if not earlier still. As a matter of fact the Chinese chronicles make definite references to maritime intercourse between India and Cambodia in the third century A.D. As we shall see later, according to local traditions preserved in a Chinese chronicle of the third century A.D. the first Hindu kingdom was founded in Southern Cambodia in the first century A.D. This date cannot in any case be very wide of the mark.

The beginnings of Indian colonies in Cambodia, like those in other parts of Indo-China, are lost in oblivion, but are echoed in local legends and traditions. These legends and traditions cannot, of course, be regarded as true chronicles of events, but they possess historical importance inasmuch as they have preserved the popular beliefs about the foundation of Hindu civilisation, and indicate in a general way the process of Hindu colonisation of these lands.

The two most important kingdoms in Cambodia in the earliest period were Fu-nan and Kambuja. Both of these had their own local legends about the beginning of Hindu colonisation. The legend current in Fu-nan as recorded by K'ang T'ai in the middle of the third century A.D. runs as follows:—

"The sovereign of Fu-nan was originally a female called Lieu-ye. There was a person called Huen-chen of Mo-fu. He was a staunch devotee of a Brahmanical god who was pleased with his piety. He dreamt that the god gave him a divine bow and asked him to take to sea in a trading vessel. In the morning he went to the temple of the god and found a bow. Then he embarked on a trading vessel and the god changed the course of wind in such a manner that he came to Fu-nan. Lieu-ye came in a boat to plunder

14. *BEFEO*. III. pp. 271-72.

the vessel. Huen-chen raised his bow and shot an arrow which pierced through the queen's boat from one side to the other The queen was overtaken by fear and submitted to him. Thereupon Huen-chen ruled over the country".[15]

The same story is repeated in later Chinese texts,[16] in some cases with additional details, such as the marriage between Huen-chen and Lieu-ye. The names of the king and queen are variously written as Huen-huei or Huen-tien and Ye–lieu. Huen-tien and Lieu–ye may be accepted as the correct forms. Huen-tien and the other variant forms represent the Indian name Kauṇḍinya. Lieu-ye probably means "Leaf of Willow".

In an inscription in the neighbouring kingdom of Champā dated 657 A.D. we find an echo of the same story. Referring to the foundation of Bhavapura, the capital of Kambuja, it says:—[17]

"It was there that Kauṇḍinya, the foremost among Brāhmaṇas, planted the spear which he had obtained from Droṇa's son Aśvatthāmā the best of Brāhmaṇas.

There was a daughter of the king of serpents, called Somā, who founded a family in this world. Having attained, through love, to a radically different element, she lived in the habitations of man.

She was taken as wife by the excellent Brāhmaṇa Kauṇḍinya for the sake of (accomplishing) certain work. Verily, incomprehensible is the way of God in providing conditions leading to future events.

(King Bhavavarman) who, being born in that pure unbroken line of kingsa is, even to-day, the pride of his subjects by his unblamable (conduct)".

We may compare this legend with the following account preserved in the Cambodian Annals about the origin of the kingdom of Cambodia[18]:—

"Ādityavaṁśa, king of Indraprastha, was displeased with one of his sons and banished him from the state. He came to the country

15. *Et As.* II, pp. 244 ff. Pelliot discusses in this connection the location of Mo-fu, the original home of Huen-chen, but is unable to come to any definite conclusion.

16. *BEFEO.* III. pp. 254, 256, 265.

17. *Champa*, Book III, p. 23.

18. *Champa*, p. XVIII.

of Kok Thlok and made himself master of it by defeating the native king. One evening he was walking on a sand bank when suddenly the tide arose and obliged him to pass the night there. A Nāgī of marvellous beauty came to play on the sand and the king, overpowered by her charm, agreed to marry her. Then the Nāgarāja, the father of the betrothed girl, extended the dominions of his would be son-in-law by drinking the water which covered the country, built a capital for him and changed the name of the kingdom into that of Kāmboja".

A somewhat different version is preserved about the origin of Kambujadeśa, in later Annals.

In the dim past, so runs the story, Cambodia was a desert of sand and rocks. One day Kambu Svāyambhuva, the king of Āryadeśa, found himself in this dreary landscape. The death of his wife Merā, whom the great god Śiva himself gave to him, made him disconsolate and he left his country "in order to die in the wildest desert" he could find. Having reached Cambodia he entered into a cave. To his horror Kambu found himself in the midst of a large number of huge, many-headed snakes, whose piercing eyes were turned towards him. Kambu, however, boldly unsheathed his sword and advanced towards the biggest snake. To the utter amazement of Kambu the snake spoke in a human voice and asked his whereabouts. On hearing Kambu's story the serpent said: "Your name is unknown to me, stranger, but you spoke of Siva, and Śiva is my king, as I am the king of the Nāgas, the great snakes. You seem to be courageous too; therefore abide with us in this land you have chosen and end your grief." Kambu remained and came to like the Nāgas who could take human shape. Several years later he married the Nāga king's daughter. The king of the Nāgas possessed magic power and turned the arid land into a beautiful country like that of Āryadeśa. Kambu ruled over the land and the kingdom came to be called after him 'Kambuja'. This mythical legend is briefly referred to in the Bakesei Cankrom Ins. dated 947 A.D., where the Kambuja kings are said to have been descended from the great sage Kambu Svāyambhuva, to whom Hara gave as wife Merā the most glorious of Apsaras.

It is interesting to note that both the mythical traditions noted above were current among the Pallavas who ruled in South India in the early centuries of the Christian Era. Thus some records describe Skandaśiṣya, the progenitor of the Pallavas, as the son of Aśvatthāmā (son of Droṇa) by a Nāga woman. Other records refer to Vīrakurcha, the predecessor of Skandaśiṣya, as having married a Nāgī and obtained from her the insignia of royalty. Manimekhalai and three other Tamil texts also mention the marriage of a Chola king and a Nāgi and their son as the Pallava king of Kāñchī. The basic factor in all these traditions viz., the origin of a royal dynasty from the marriage of an Indian prince with a Nāga woman, is thus similar to the traditions current in Fu-nan, and what is more striking, the mythical Aśvatthāmā is associated, though in different rôle, in both cases. The tradition may, however, be carried still further back. For Herodotus records a similar story about the progenitor of the Scythians. Heracles, we are told, met in Scythia a strange creature, the upper part of whose body was that of a woman but the lower part that of a serpent. She bore three sons to Heracles, who left instructions before his departure that whichever of these three could bend the bow left by him, should be made the king of the country. According to this test Scythe became the ruler and his descendants were called after him Scythians. Apart from general resemblance the episode of the bow, contained in it, offers the common element with one version of the Fu-nan tradition preserved in Chinese texts. Whether the common tradition about the origin of the royal dynasty proves any close connection between the people of Fu-nan and the Pallavas on the one hand, and between the Pallavas and the Scythians on the other, is a speculative problem, which it is unnecessary to discuss for our present purpose. We must, however, note that there is also a Pallava parallel to the second tradition of Kambuja which derives the royal dynasty from the sage, Kambu Svyāmbhuva, to whom the God Śiva gave as wife the most glorious Apsarā named Merā. The Pallava story as recorded in a Sanskrit inscription found at Amaravati runs as follows. "By the favour of Śiva, Droṇa had a glorious son named Aśvatthāmā who became an ascetic, and lived in a forest. One day the Apsarā Madani came to his hermitage, and both became enamoured of each other. The Apsarā bore him a son named Pallava, who became the originator of the dynasty known after him." Here also we find this common basic theme, viz., the origin of the royal dynasty by the union between a sage and an Apsarā, though the rôle played by Śiva is slightly different. The mention of Aśvatthāmā is also interesting inasmuch as he figures in the other tradition.[19]

19. *BEFEO*. XI, pp. 391-93; XXIV, pp. 501 ff.

Whatever we might think of these traditions as a connecting link between the Indian colonists in Cambodia and a known region or a ruling dynasty in India, they have undoubtedly some historical value, for we cannot fail to note in them an allegorical representation of the conquest of the land of primitive wild tribes (Nāgas) by the colonists from India (Āryadeśa) who introduced the elements of higher civilisation among the primitive aborigines. The introduction of names like Kambu and Śiva is no doubt due to the dominance of Śaivism.

Whether the same band of colonists spread over the whole of Cambodia or its different parts were colonised by different groups of immigrants at different times cannot be definitely decided. Nor is it quite certain whether all the immigrants came direct from India or some of them at any rate came from other Indian colonial kingdoms. The probability is that a number of small states were founded in different parts of Cambodia by groups of people coming at different times both from India and Indian colonies in the neighbourhood. The names of some of these states which acknowledged the suzerainty of Fu-nan are preserved in Chinese chronicles.

The History of the Liang Dynasty (502-556 A.D.) gives us the following account of Tuen-siun.

"In the southern frontier of Fu-nan, at a distance of more than 3,000 *li* lies the kingdom of Tuen-siun on a rugged sea-shore. It is about 1000 *li* in extent. The capital city is about 10 *li* from the sea. There are five kings, all of whom are vassals of Fu-nan. The merchants from India and Parthia came in large numbers to carry on trade and commerce, the reason being that Tuen-siun forms a curve projecting into the sea for more than a thousand *li*. The sea[20] is vast and without limit and cannot be crossed directly.[21] Hence the market of Tuen-siun forms a meeting ground between the east and the west, frequented every day by more than ten

20. The Chinese name Chang-hai refers to the Sea of China extending from Hai-nan to the Malay Peninsula. It includes the Gulf of Tonkin (BEFEO. III, p. 263, f.n. 2).

21. As Pelliot observes, the Chinese text is somewhat obscure. Both Pelliot and Schlegel are of opinion that the Chinese vessels did not directly cross the sea from Annamese coast to the Malay Peninsula. They consequently followed the coast line and probably the goods were transhipped across the isthmus of Kra, thereby saving a lot of time. There is, however, no definite evidence in support of this view (BEFEO. III, p. 263 f.n. 3—cf., *Suvarnadvipa*, I. pp. 85-6).

thousand men. Rare objects, precious merchandises, in short everything is found there. Moreover there is a tree, resembling pomegranate-tree, the juice of whose flowers is collected in a jar and, after a few days, is transformed into wine".[22]

An Indian, named Che by the Chinese, who lived in the fifth century A.D.[23] and visited these parts gives the following account of Tuen-siun.

"Tuen-siun is a vassal state of Fu-nan. The king is called Kuen-Luen. It contains five hundred Hu (probably of mercantile caste) families of India, two *hundred* Fo-tu (probably Buddhists),[24] and more than thousand Brahmans of India. The people of Tuen-siun follow their religion and give them their daughters in marriage, as most of these Brahmans settle in the country and do not go away. Day and night they read sacred scriptures and make offerings of white vases, perfumes and flowers to the gods. When they fall ill they take a vow to be devoured by the birds. They are led outside the town to the accompaniment of music and dance, and they are left to be devoured by the birds. The bones are then burnt and put in a jar which is thrown into the sea. If the birds do not devour them, they are placed in a basket. The "cremation by fire" consists in throwing the body into fire. The ashes are collected in a vase which is buried, and to which sacrifices are made for an unlimited period".[25] (It then refers to preparation of wine as in the previous extract).

The account of Tuen-siun is very illuminating as it gives a vivid image of an Indian colony in a foreign land, and shows the process by which Indian colonies grew and exerted their influence over the indigenous population. It is the usual story of trade followed by a missionary propaganda, both Brahmanical and Buddhist, of gradual settlement of Indians in the country, and ultimate fusion with the people by intermarriage with the native population.

Like Tuen-siun Fu-nan itself was an important market town where met the traders from India and China. Evidently the same process, as described above, did also operate here in making it a

22. *BEFEO*. III, p. 263.

23. *BEFEO*. III, p. 277.

24. Fo-tu means Buddha as well as *Stūpa*. The figure is two, possibly a mistake for two hundred (*Ibid*, p. 279 f.n. 5).

25. *Ibid*, p. 279.

flourishing Indian colony. Its supremacy was perhaps due to the fact that Indian colonists seized the political power at an early stage.

References are not wanting in Chinese texts to communication between Fu-nan and India. The story of Kia-sing-li, who came from India to Fu-nan in course of trade, will be mentioned later. Reference has already been made to the fact that during the period 147-167 A.D. several Indian embassies went to China through the Southern seas. As the vessels in those days kept close to the coast, Fu-nan must have been an important halting station in this voyage. The new History of the Tang dynasty (618-906 A.D.) refers to exchange of diamonds, sandals and other goods between India on the one hand and Fu-nan and Kiao-che (Tonkin) on the other.[26] Another Chinese text says that a big vessel of Fu-nan coming from western India had for sale a mirror of blue po-li (*sphaṭika*) which had a diameter of 16 ft. 5 inches and weighed more than forty pounds.[27]

We may thus easily visualise the process by which Fu-nan and other Indian colonies were founded in Cambodia. In course of time Fu-nan grew more powerful than others and established its sway over the whole of Cambodia and even far beyond its frontier. Fortunately we possess a somewhat detailed account of its rise and development, and this will form the subject of my next lecture.

26. *Ibid*, p. 275.
27. *Ibid*, p. 283.

LECTURE II

THE KINGDOM OF FU-NAN

The earliest historical account of the Khmers is bound up with the kingdom of Fu-nan, which is frequently referred to in the Chinese texts from the third to the seventh century A.D. Strangely enough, all traditions of the kingdom, and even its very name, disappeared after the seventh century A.D. without leaving any trace. The location of this kingdom became, therefore, a matter of considerable difficulty, and various opinions about it were expressed by different scholars. To M. Paul Pelliot belongs the credit of finally settling this question and also of collecting together the historical information about this kingdom scattered in different Chinese texts. The following account of the kingdom of Fu-nan is mainly based on the materials collected by him on the subject.[1]

The name of the kingdom, Fu-nan, is written in different ways by the Chinese, and I–tsing calls it Pa-nan. M. Aymonier regards it as a pure Chinese word meaning 'the protected south,' but Pelliot infers from the different forms of the name, that it is merely a Chinese transcription of an original name. Unfortunately, this original name cannot be restored with any amount of certainty. The views of Schlegel and Parker that the original name was P'o-nam or Phnom (—penh) are rejected by Pelliot.[2] G. Coedès derives the name from Ba Phnom, a region round the hill of that name in South Cambodia,[3] and this seems to be the most plausible view.

The kingdom of Fu-nan corresponded roughly to Cambodia proper and a part of Cochin–China, and comprised the lower valley of the Mekong. The capital of this kingdom, according to some Chinese texts, was 500 *li* from the sea. If, as it seems very probable, this distance was measured by the route along the Mekong river, the capital must have been situated between Chaudoc and

1. Cf. "Le Fou-Nan" by P. Pelliot in *BEFEO*. Vol. III, pp. 248-303. In the following foot-notes of this chapter, the pages, unless otherwise indicated, refer to this article.

2. P. 288.

3. *BEFEO*. Vol. XXVIII, pp. 129-30.

Phnom Penh, a region which was once the centre of Khmer civilisation. Pelliot, following Aymonier, infers from an inscription found in the province of Battambang that the earliest capital of the historical kingdom of Kambuja which replaced Fu-nan was most probably Vyādhapura. He identifies it with modern Angkorbaurei, and thinks it very likely that it was also the capital of Fu-nan. Coedès, however, rejects this view. He locates Vyādhapura at the foot of the peak at Ba Phnom and regards it as the capital of Fu-nan, though not of Kambujadeśa.[5]

According to the Chinese account the primitive people of Fu-nan were semi-savages. They went about naked and decorated themselves with tattoo marks.[6] Their queen Lieu-ye was, however, defeated by Huen-tien, a follower of the Brahmanical religion, who introduced the elements of civilised life. In particular he made the women wear clothes.[7]

This Huen-tien was most probably a Hindu colonist who came direct from India, though the possibility is not altogether excluded that he might have been a Hinduised colonist from some part of Malay Peninsula or Malay Archipelago.[8] From the accounts of subsequent events[9] his arrival cannot be placed later than the first century A.D. No particulars of Huen-tien's reign are known to us,[10] but his son is said to have been given an appanage of seven towns[11]. The existence or creation of these vassal states was not without danger to the kingdom. However, one of the successors of Huen-tien, named Huen P'an-huang, sowed the seeds of disunion among the seven towns and thus succeeded in bringing them under his control. Then he appointed his sons and grandsons as

4. P. 290.

5. *BEFEO*. Vol. XXVIII, pp. 127-131.

6. P. 265.

7. P. 256. See *ante* p. 17.

8. *Cf. Et. As.* II, pp. 245-46, where Pelliot discusses the location of Mo-fu, the original home of Huen-chen (pp. 247-66), but is unable to come to any definite conclusion.

9. These are referred to below.

10. Except, of course, his civilising mission referred to above.

11. Cf. p. 265. The passage is somewhat obscure, though this seems to be the proper meaning. It is evident from what follows that the governors of the seven towns grew to be too powerful for the central authority and it was only by creating dissensions among them that they were once more brought under control.

governors of only a single town. They were called 'small kings'[12] Huen P'an-huang, as the first part of the name indicates, was undoubtedly a descendant of Huen–tien,[13] and ruled during the second half of the second century A.D.

Huen P'an-huang died at the advanced age of ninety and was succeeded by his second son P'an–p'an. He left the cares of government to his great general Fan-man, or Fan–che–man. When the king died after a reign of three years Fan–che–man was elected king by the people[14] (c. 200 A.D.).

Fan-che-man was an able ruler and laid the foundation of the greatness of Fu-nan. He constructed a powerful navy and conquered the neighbouring states to a distance of five or six thousand *li* which henceforth became vassals of Fu-nan. Although the Chinese names of these vassal states cannot all be satisfactorily identified, we may hold in a general way that nearly the whole of Siam and parts of Laos and Malay Peninsula acknowledged the authority of Fu-nan which thus became the first Hindu colonial empire in Indo-China. Fan-che-man assumed the title 'Great king of Fu-nan' and was about to lead a campaign against Kin-lin (Suvarṇabhūmi or Suvarnadvīpa) when he fell ill and died. During his illness he had sent his eldest son Fan-Kin-cheng to take charge of the army, but the general Fan Chan, son of the elder sister of Fan–che–man, taking advantage of the absence of Fan–Kin-cheng, declared himself king and put Fan–Kin–cheng to death (c. 225 A.D.).[15]

The reign of Fan Chan is of special importance as we know definitely that he sent embassies to both China and India. According to *San Kuo Che* (which deals with the history of the period from 220 to 280 A.D. and was written towards the end of the third cen-

12. P. 265.

13. This also clearly follows from the statement in the History of the Southern Tsi Dynasty that the sons and grandsons of Huen-tien ruled the country up to the death of P'an-huang (pp. 256-7).

14. P. 265.

15. *Cf.* p. 266-7 and the footnotes. For Kin-lin cf. p. 266 f.n. (5). It was about two thousand *li* from Fu-nan. The people were Buddhist and there were several thousand *śramaṇas* in the country. The Chinese Kin-lin means 'frontier of cold' but it is sometimes identified with Kin-chen which means island of gold. The Chinese name may, therefore, be regarded as equivalent to Suvarnabhūmi or Suvarnadvīpa. On the identification of this cf. my book *Suvarnadvipa*, Part I pp. 37 ff.

tury A.D. by Chen Chen) Fan Chan, king of Fu–nan, sent an embassy to China in 243 A.D., offering as presents a few musicians and some products of the country.[16] This is one of the earliest references to official relationship between China and Fu–nan.[17] Incidentally it gives us the first fixed point in the chronology of the kings of Fu–nan, on the basis of which it has been possible to assign approximate dates to the previous kings.

A Chinese text of the third century A.D. tells us that Kia-sing–li, an inhabitant of T'an–Yang, in the western part of India, made voyages for purposes of trade and ultimately reached Fu-nan during the reign of Fan Chan. He gave the king a graphic description of the laws, manners, customs, and the immense wealth of India. Being asked the distance, he said it was 30,000 *li*, and a return voyage from Fu-nan would take three to four years.[18] Fan Chan's curiosity was perhaps aroused by these stories. In any case he sent one of his relations named Su-Wu as an ambassador to India. Su–Wu embarked at Teu–ki–li, probably the famous port of Takkola, and reached the mouth of the great river of India (Ganges) after about a year. Having proceeded up the river for 7,000 *li*, he met the king of India. The latter cordially welcomed Su-Wu and arranged for his visit to the different parts of the kingdom. He sent two envoys to accompany Su-Wu to the king of Fu–nan with a present of four horses of Yu–che country, and these came to Fu–nan four years after Su-Wu had left the country.[19]

These four years, however, witnessed great political changes. King Fan Chan was no longer on the throne of Fu-nan. He was assassinated by Fan Chang, a younger son of Fan-che-man. Fan Chang was a baby at the time of his father's death, but when he was twenty years old, he collected a few brave persons and killed Fan Chan in order to avenge the murder of his elder brother. It is not definitely known whether Fan Chang ascended the throne, but even if he did so, his reign must have been short. He was

16. P. 303.

17. Pelliot says on p. 303 that this is the earliest embassy, but on p. 233 he refers to a passage from Wu-li to the effect that Fu-nan sent an embassy to China in 225 A.D. (or, according to another version of the same passage of Wu-ll, quoted by a later writer, during the period 229-31 A.D.)

18. P. 277.

19. P. 271.

assassinated by the general Fan Siun who succeeded him as king of Fu-nan.[20]

It was during the reign of Fan Siun, probably some time between 245 and 250 A.D., that the Chinese ambassadors K'ang T'ai and Chu Ying visited Fu-nan. It was evidently in recognition of the embassy sent by him to China. The Chinese ambassadors met in Fu-nan Chen-song, one of the envoys sent by the king of India.

This Chinese embassy is of more than passing importance to Fu-nan. K'ang T'ai and Chu Ying wrote two books on Fu-nan which gave to the Chinese the first authentic account of the kingdom and supplied the main source of information to later writers on the subject.[21] In particular K'ang T'ai's work is frequently referred to by later authors. He may be compared to Magasthenes, and it is of tragic interest to note that like the Indica of the latter, K'ang T'ai's work is lost and only fragments of it are preserved in quotations by later authors. It may be added that K'ang T'ai also recorded a brief account of India as reported by Chen-song.

The only point of importance in this account of India is that it gives us more detailed information about the particular kingdom in India visited by the envoy of Fu-nan. According to the statement of Chen-song, as reported by K'ang-T'ai, 'the title of his king was Meu-lun and to the right and left of his kingdoms, there were six great kingdoms, *viz.*, those of Kia-wei (Kapilāvastu), Che-Wei (Śrāvastī) etc. This leaves no doubt that the great river of India through which the envoy of Fu-nan proceeded inland for 7,000 *li* was the Ganges, and that the kingdom he visited was situated somewhere in U.P. M. Sylvain Lévi has proposed the identification of Meu-lun with the Murundas. This dynasty is referred to in the Purāṇas as having ruled for 350 years, but there is no indication about the locality of their kingdom. A Jaina work refers to Pāṭaliputra as the residence of a Muruṇda-rāja, but it is not clear whether it is a personal (cf. Śiśunāga king Muṇḍa) or a tribal name. The Muruṇdas are also referred to in the Allahabad Pillar inscription of Samudragupta, but it is extremely improbable that they could have ruled anywhere in the upper Ganges valley at the time of that great emperor. S. Lévi's hypothesis that the envoy of Fu-nan visited the kingdom of the Muruṇdas near about Pāṭali-

20. P. 267.
21. P. 275.

putra, is at best a plausible, though very doubtful one, and all that we can safely assert is that Fu-nan's ambassador visited a kingdom on the upper Ganges valley.

As regards K'ang Tai's account of Fu-nan, the only point that need be referred to at present is his observation that though the country is beautiful, it is strange that the men went about naked. King Fan Siun, however, stopped this indecent habit.[22]

Fan Siun had a long reign and sent several embassies to China in the years 268, 285, 286 and 287 A.D.[23] An interesting sidelight is thrown on the political status of Fu-nan about this time by the memorandum prepared by T'ao Huang, the governor of Tonkin, when the emperor expressed a desire to reduce the military expenditure. T'ao Huang prayed that the garrison of Tonkin which formerly consisted of 7,000, and now only 2420, men should not be reduced any further. As a reason for this he pointed out the danger of constant incursions of Fan Hiong, the ruler of Champā. Further, he said, that the Chams and the people of the adjoining country Fu-nan are allies, and the two support each other. Their tribes are numerous and they don't submit to China.[24]

The next reference to Fu-nan in Chinese history is in connection with an embassy sent in A.D. 357 by a Hindu named Chantan.[25] According to the Chinese texts this Hindu took the title of the King of Fu-nan. This indicates a period of political troubles with several claimants for the throne. The name of the Hindu may be restored as Chandana or Chandra.[26] He sent a petition and presented some tamed elephants to the Chinese king. The latter, however, issued an order to the effect that as the maintenance of these animals entails considerable expenditure they should not be sent as presents.[27] According to other texts the emperor considered these strange animals as sources of evil to the people and ordered them to be returned.[28]

22. P. 268.
23. P. 252.
24. P. 255.
25. Pp. 252-3, 255, 289.
26. S. Lévi restores the name as Cinasthāna equivalent to Devaputra, and regards it as a title of the king of India who in his opinion sent this embassy. (Melanges Charles de Harlez, pp. 176 ff). Pelliot rejects this view (p. 252 f.n. 4).
27. P. 269.
28. P. 255.

Towards the end of the fourth or the beginning of the fifth century A.D. the throne of Fu-nan was occupied by Kiao-chen-ju or Kauṇḍinya. The History of the Liang Dynasty has preserved the following story about him: "Kauṇḍinya was a Brahman and an inhabitant of India. One day he heard a supernatural voice asking him to go and reign in Fu-nan. He reached P'an-p'an to the south of Fu-nan. The people of Fu-nan cordially welcomed him and elected him king. He introduced Indian laws, manners and customs."[29] This story perhaps preserves an echo of a fresh stream of colonists coming direct from India, as a result of which the country was thoroughly Hinduised.

Next we hear of Ch'e-li-t'o-pa-mo, a successor of Kauṇḍinya sending embassies, with presents, to the Imperial Court in 434, 435 and 438 A.D.[30]

The History of the First Song dynasty which gives us the above information also tells us that in the year 431 or 432 A.D. the king of Champā, intending to overthrow Tonkin, asked for military aid from the king of Fu-nan, but the latter refused the request.[31] The king of Fu-nan was most probably Ch'e-li-t'o-pa-mo.

The Chinese texts tell us a great deal more about another successor of Kauṇḍinya.[32]

Towards the close of the Song period (420-478 A.D.) king Chö-ye-pa-mo (Jayavarman) ruled in Fu-nan. His family name was Kauṇḍinya. He sent some merchants to Canton for purposes of trade. On their return journey the Indian monk Na-kia-sien (Nā-gasena) joined them for coming back to his country. But a storm forced them to land in Champā whose people plundered all their goods. Nāgasena, however, reached Fu-nan. a

In A.D. 484 Jayavarman sent Nāgasena to the imperial court with a long petition, the full text of which is given in the Chinese chronicles. After the usual compliments and expressions of good will it refers to the disastrous voyage of Nāgasena and the merchants from Canton in course of which they were robbed by the

29. P. 269.

30. *The History of the first Song Dynasty* which refers to the embassies in detail gives the name of the king as Ch'e-li-pa-mo. (p. 255). *The History of the Liang Dynasty* gives the name as Che-li-to-pa-mo (p.

31. P. 255.

32. Pp. 257-261.

king of Champā. It then refers to the glowing account of the laws, religion and the government of China given by Nāgasena which induced Jayavarman to send his humble presents and ask for the good wishes of the emperor.

The petition then narrates in detail how a rebellious subject of Fu-nan, named Kieu-ch'eu-lo fled to Champā, organised a rebellion there and made himself master of Champā. He was there indulging in all sorts of violence and injustice, and what was worse, adopted an attitude of open hostility against the king of Fu-nan, his original master. As Fu-nan and Champā had a common boundary, Jayavarman was naturally anxious to get rid of him and asked the emperor to send a force against Champā, which he complacently described as originally a vassal state of China. He offered to help the imperial troops in their task of subjugating Champā, and agreed to recognise, as King of Champā, any other person nominated by the emperor. Even if the emperor were unwilling to send a powerful army to chastise the king of Champā, Jayavarman requested him to send a small force to help him in punishing the wicked king. In order to strengthen his case he sent rich presents including a golden model of the throne of Nāga-rāja, an elephant of white sandal, two ivory *stūpas,* two pieces of cotton, two vases of precious transparent stones, and a betel-nut plate made of shell.

Nāgasena proceeded to the imperial capital and gave an account of the manners and customs of Fu-nan, the most interesting point in which is a reference to the dominant cult of Maheśvara, the god who lives on the Motan hill. He also presented a poem, which is somewhat abstruse but evidently eulogises the god Maheśvara, Buddha and the emperor.

The emperor praised the god Maheśvara and condemned the wicked usurper of the throne of Champā. But then he added: "It is only by the culture and virtue that I attract the distant people, but I do not like to have recourse to arms. However, according to the established convention of the government, I am referring the request of the king of Fu-nan for military assistance against Champā to a tribunal." The decision of the tribunal is not on record, but there is nothing to show that any military assistance was given. The emperor, however, presented a large quantity of silk of various colours to the king of Fu-nan.

In 503 A.D. Jayavarman again sent an embassy to the imperial court with presents including an image of Buddha, made of coral. On this occasion the following imperial edict was issued: "The king of Fu-nan Kauṇḍinya Jayavarman lives on the border of the ocean. For generations he and his forefathers have ruled over that distant country of the south and their sincerity (of respectful feelings to the emperor) is manifested by frequent embassies and presents. It is proper to show some favour in return and to bestow a grand title upon him. Hence (I confer) the title "The General of the pacified south, the king of Fu-nan."[33]

Jayavarman sent two more embassies to the imperial court, one in 511 and the other in 514 A.D.[34] There is no doubt that throughout his reign a very cordial and intimate relation subsisted between the two countries. This is further proved by the fact that two Buddhist monks of Fu-nan settled in China[35] whose works are still preserved in the Tripiṭaka. One of them, Saṅghapāla or Saṅghavarman (460-524 A.D.), knew several languages, and spent sixteen years (506-522) in translating, at the command of the emperor Wu, various canonical texts in five different places. One of these was called Fu-nan-Kuan or Bureau of Fu-nan.

The second monk was named Mandra or Mandrasena. He arrived at the imperial capital in A.D. 503, and was commanded by the emperor Wu to collaborate with Saṅghapāla in the translation of sacred scriptures.

Jayavarman died in A.D. 514. His elder son, Rudravarman, born of a concubine, succeeded him after having killed the younger son born of his legitimate wife. An inscription found at Neak Ta Dambang Dek in the province of Treang[36] in southern Cambodia refers to the foundation of a hermitage (*ārāma*) with a tank and a dwelling house (*ālaya*) by queen Kulaprabhāvatī, the principal spouse of a king called Jayavarman. In view of the palaeography and find-spot of the Ins. Coedès, who edited it, has identified this king with Jayavarman of Fu-nan. The alphabet of this inscription bears a close resemblance with that of the Thap Musi Ins.[37] of Guṇavarman, who is described as the young son of a king of the family of Kauṇḍinya. Coedés suggests on the joint evidence of these two inscriptions that the young Gunavarman was the son of Jayavarman and Kulaprabhāvatī, and his legitimate succession to

33. P. 269.
34. P. 270.
35. Pp. 284-5.
36. Edited by Coedès, *JGIS*, IV. pp. 117 ff.
37. *BEFEO*. XXXI, pp. 1 ff.

the throne was prevented by Rudravarman. This is a very reasonable hypothesis, but cannot be regarded as an established fact until further evidence is available.

Rudravarman is also referred to in an epigraphic record.[38] A Buddhist inscription, sadly mutilated, belongs to his reign, and eulogises his royal qualities. It refers to the appointment of an official by his father Jayavarman, but does not give us any historical information.

Rudravarman sent no less than six embassies to China in 517, 519, 520, 530, 535 and 539 A.D. The envoy sent in 517 was an Indian named Tang-pao-lao (Dharmapāla?). The presents sent in 519 included an image of Buddha made of Indian sandalwood, and pearls or precious stones of India. In 539 he sent a living rhinoceros and offered to the emperor a hair of Buddha 12 ft. long which was in his country. The emperor sent a monk to fetch the precious relic.[33a]

Rudravarman is the last king of Fu-nan referred to by name in the Chinese texts. Nothing is known of this kingdom during the next three quarters of a century. But we learn from the Chinese chronicles that Fu-nan was conquered by Citrasena king of Chen-la, whose son Īśānasena sent an embassy to the Chinese court in 616-7 A.D.[39] It is obvious, however, that the conquest by Chitrasena did not mean an end of the kingdom of Fu-nan. For we learn from the Chinese texts that T'ö-mu, the capital of Fu-nan, was suddenly seized by Chen-la, and the king of Fu-nan removed himself to a town called Na-fu-na, further to the south.[40] According to Pelliot the Chinese name may stand for Navanagara, and this city was probably situated somewhere near Kampot.[41] Further, the Chinese texts refer to two embassies of Fu-nan in the first half of the seventh century A.D.[42] The last reference to Fu-nan occurs in the account of I-tsing (671-695 A.D.) in the following words:—

38. *Ibid.*

38a. Pp. 270-1.

39. P. 272. It is not expressly stated that Īśānasena sent the embassy, but that is the obvious inference as he is referred to as the reigning king.

40. P. 274.

41. P. 295.

42. One between 618 and 626 A.D., and the other between 627 and 649 A.D. (p. 274).

"Leaving Champā and going towards the south-west the country of Pa-nan is reached. Formerly this was called Fu-nan. In ancient times it was the country of the naked men. The people worshipped many Devas. Then the law of Buddha prospered and expanded. But at the present time a wicked king has completely destroyed it and there are no more monks."[43]

It may be surmised from the above that some vestiges of the ancient kingdom of Fu-nan survived till the end of the seventh century A.D.

The name Chen-la is used by the Chinese to refer to the kingdom of Kambuja. The inscriptions of Cambodia give us a detailed and connected account of the kingdom from the seventh century A.D. Even the two kings of Chen-la, referred to above, are known from these inscriptions. There can be hardly any doubt that Kambuja was originally a vassal state of Fu-nan that grew powerful enough in the seventh century A.D. to assert its supremacy and destroy the suzerain power.[44] Henceforth Kambuja takes the place of Fu-nan and continues a glorious existence for nearly seven hundred years. But before proceeding to deal with the history of this powerful kingdom we should make a broad review of the kingdom of Fu-nan, the first Hindu kingdom in Cambodia, if not in Indo-China, and trace the development of its culture and civilisation on the basis of the data supplied by the Chinese chronicles.

The early history of Fu-nan is a repetition of that of almost every ancient Hindu colony in the Far East. Originally a country of savages or semi-barbarians, it imbibes the element of civilisation from a Hindu or Hinduised chief who establishes his authority either by conquest or by more peaceful methods. Gradually it comes more and more into direct contact with India and Hindu culture and civilisation become the dominant feature.

In the case of Fu-nan we can distinctly trace two broad stages of Indianisation, one in the first and another in the fourth century A.D., and in both cases under the influence of its rulers, whose names are supposed to represent the same Indian name, Kauṇḍinya. The earlier, Huen-tien, is said to have followed the Brahmanical cult, but there is no definite information of his original home. Naturally one might be tempted to regard him as coming direct

43. Takakusu-I-tsing, p. 10.
44. This will be more fully dealt with in the next Lecture.

from India. But the story of the Indian merchant Kia-siang-li who visited the court of king Fan Chan seems to militate against this view. For, if we believe in the details of the story it would appear that the king had never heard of India before. But such stories are not to be taken too literally, and perhaps the sentiments of the Chinese writer, to whom India was a *terra incognita,* rather than those of the king and people of Fu-nan, have been reflected in them. For the Chinese texts tell us that during the time of the emperor Huan of the later Han dynasty (147-167 A.D.) Indian embassies came to China by the southern sea and they must have passed by Fu-nan. According to the same texts, however, this political intercourse completely ceased in the third century A.D.[45] This might account for the ignorance of India in the Far East in the third century A.D., but as the story of Huen-tien goes back to the first century A.D. there is no inherent improbability in the very natural assumption that he came from India. We have, therefore, good reason to believe that the first Hindu colonists from India settled in Fu-nan not later than the first century A.D.

There is, however, no doubt that Kauṇḍiṇya of the fourth century A.D. came direct from India, as this is explicitly stated in the Chinese Texts.

The first reference to the people of Fu-nan occurs in a poem composed in the third century A.D. by Tso-Sseu. He says that the people of Fu-nan[46] are clever and should not be confused with the barbarians.

The earliest general account of Fu–nan is given in the *History of the Tsin Dynasty* which covers the period from 265 to 419 A.D. and was composed by Fang Hiuan-ling (578-648 A.D.). It runs as follows:—

"The kingdom of Fu-nan is more than 3,000 *li* to the west of Lin-yi (Champā) in a great bay of the ocean. The country is three thousand *li* in extent. There are many walled towns, palaces, and houses. The people are black and ugly. They have curly hair and go about naked and bare footed. Their nature is simple and they are not at all given to theft or robbery. They apply themselves to agriculture. They sow one year and gather harvest during next three years. Moreover they love to engrave and

45. Pp. 271, 272.
46. P. 281.

chisel their ornaments. They mostly take their food on silver plates. The taxes are paid in gold, silver, pearls and perfumes. They have many books and there are libraries and archives. In writing they use an alphabet derived from India.[47] Their funeral and marriage ceremonies are like those of Champā".[48]

The following account is preserved in the *History of the Southern Ts'i* covering the period from 479 to 501 and composed at the beginning of the sixth century A.D.

"The people of Fu-nan are crafty and malicious. They forcibly carry away and reduce to slavery the inhabitants of the neighbouring towns that do not submit to their authority. Their articles of trade are gold, silver, and silk. The men of noble families use *Sarong* made of brocade. The females cover their body in a dress that passes over their head. The poor people cover their bodies with a piece of cloth. The inhabitants of Fu-nan use golden rings and bracelets and silver vessels. They cut woods to make their houses. The king lives in a storeyed pavilion. The houses are enclosed by a wooden palisade. The houses are sometimes covered by bamboo-leaves, 8 or 9 ft. long. They also live in houses raised above the ground. They construct boats 80 to 90 ft. long and 6 or 7 ft. wide, the front and back of which are shaped like the head and tail of a fish. When the king goes out he rides on an elephant. The women also ride on elephants. They arrange cock-fight and pig-fight for their amusements. They have no prison. In case of dispute they throw a golden ring or egg in boiling water and the disputants have to draw them out or they have to walk seven steps carrying red-hot iron chain in their hands. The hands of the guilty are completely burnt, but the innocent do not suffer any injury. Sometimes the disputants are thrown into water. The guilty sinks but the innocent does not. The country produces sugar-cane, pomegranate, orange and much areca-nut. The birds and the mamalions are the same as in China. The character of the people is good and they do not like war".[49]

47. The actual words are "their characters resemble those of Hu". But as Pelliot points out (p. 254, f.n. 2), that although the Hu, properly speaking, mean the people of Central Asia, all alphabets related to those of India are included in the Hu alphabet. That the Indian alphabet was used in Fu-nan is definitely proved by the discovery of the Sanskrit inscriptions referred to in f.n. 36-38 above.

48. P. 254.

49. Pp. 261-2.

The beginning and the end of this account give us somewhat contradictory ideas about the general disposition of the people. Either they refer to different types of people living in the same country, or put together observations made by different persons, perhaps at different times.

The *History of the Liang dynasty* (502-556 A.D.) repeats much of the above information but also adds something new. The products of the country are said to be gold, silver, copper, tin, aloe, ivory, peacock, kingfisher and parrots of five colours. It adds a few details about the trial by ordeal referred to above. We are told that crocodiles are kept in the ditches outside the walls, and ferocious animals are placed inside an enclosure outside the city gates. The persons accused of criminal acts are thrown in the ditches and the enclosure, and kept for three days. If they are not devoured, they are considered innocent. In all cases the suspected persons are made to fast and practise abstinence for three days before being subjected to the ordeal.

The big crocodiles are said to have been more than 20 ft. long. They resembled the alligators, had four legs and their mouths, six or seven feet long, had on each side teeth pointed like swords. They lived ordinarily on fish, but would devour a buck or a man if they could get it.[50]

It gives the following account of the manners and customs of the people: —

"They do not sink wells in their houses, several dozens of families having a common pond whence they draw their water. They worship the spirits of heaven and make their images in bronze. Some of these have two and four faces with respectively four and eight hands. Each hand holds something, a child, a bird, an animal, sun or moon.

"The king and his concubines who live in the palace ride on elephants when going out or coming in. When the king sits, he squats on a side, with the right knee raised high and the left knee touching the ground. In front of him is spread a piece of cotton cloth, and vases of gold and burning incense are placed on it.

"In case of mourning the custom is to shave the beard and the hair. The dead are disposed of in four ways, the dead body being

50. Pp. 263, 268.

either burnt, thrown in a river, buried in the ground, or left in the field for being devoured by birds.

"The people are greedy by nature. The boys and girls mix promiscuously and they observe neither ceremony nor decency."[51]

The *New History of the T'ang dynasty* (618-906) refers to a kind of diamond produced in the country. In appearance it is like quartz. It is found in abundance on rocks deep under water and the people dive into water to collect them. A jade can be scratched by it, but it is broken if struck by a corner of a battering ram.[52]

Another Chinese text, *Wai Kuo Chuan*, refers to a new type of trial by ordeal. If anything is stolen in a house, a small quantity of rice is taken in a temple and the god is requested to find out the thief. The rice is placed near the feet of the god. Next day the rice is taken and the servants of the house are asked to eat it. The innocent swallows it without any difficulty, but blood comes out of the mouth of the guilty.

The same text tells us that the people of Fu-nan are noble and wealthy, and decorate their houses with sculpture. They are generous and charitable and have many birds and animals. The king is fond of hunting. They all ride on elephants and spend days and months in hunting excursions.[53]

The *Tong-tien*, a text of the nature of an Encyclopaedia, composed at the end of the eighth century, contains the following passage:

"In the time of the Suei (581-618 A.D.) the king had the family name Ku–long. There were many others in the kingdom having the same family name. The old people, when interrogated, says that the K'uen-luen (Malays) have no family name. (The Ku-long) is a corruption of K'uen-luen."[54]

The accounts culled above from the Chinese texts leave no doubt that the people of Fu-nan had imbibed Hindu culture and civilisation to a very large extent. The dominant religion was Saivism as we learn from the account of Nagasena, though Buddhism

51. P. 266.
52. P. 274.
53. P. 280.
54. P. 283.

was not unknown. The images of gods with two or four faces and four or eight hands undoubtedly refer to Brahmanical gods. Some of their manners and customs, such as putting on clothes, riding on elephants, funeral ceremonies, trial by ordeal, the luxurious mode of living as indicated by their decorated houses, costly ornaments and utensils, the royal pomp and grandeur,[55] the peculiar shape of their boats, and the title Fan (equivalent to Varman) borne by the kings all indicate an Indian influence. Their alphabets were also derived from India.

The traces of primitive barbarism were no doubt still to be found among a large section of people. This perhaps explains some of the contradictory statements in Chinese accounts. For while some say that they had marriage ceremonies like those prevalent in Champā, others refer to the promiscuous relation between boys and girls and want of a sense of decorum and decency among the people. Again, as we have already noted above, the same account which praises the good character and pacific disposition of the people, also refers to their ferocious and violent character. All these seem to indicate that although the people generally gave up their primitive nomadic habits and barbaric customs and took to agriculture, they had not all imbibed the culture and civilisation introduced by the Hindu colonists to the same degree. This is only natural, and the same phenomena are observed in other Hindu colonies e.g. Champā and Java. The main credit of the Hindu colonists lies in the great contrast between the primitive barbarism of the people whose men and women went about naked, and the highly developed culture and civilisation that flourished in the same soil after the settlement of the Hindus.

But the best evidence of the extent to which Indian culture was imbibed by the people is furnished by the three Sanskrit inscriptions of Fu-nan.[56] The first begins with an invocation to God Viṣṇu. The second records a donation by prince Guṇavarman to the image of God Viṣṇu called Cakratīrthasvāmī which was consecrated by the Brāhmaṇas versed in the Vedas, Upavedas and Vedāṅgas and sages versed in the Śruti. The third records a donation to some Buddhist establishment and refers to Buddha,

55. *The History of the Liang Dynasty* tells us that king Fan Siun constructed pavilions and belvederes and held three or four audiences a day (pp. 267-8).

50. For these inscriptions cf. f.n. 36-38 above.

Dharma and Saṅgha. The Bhāgavatas are mentioned in the second and the Āryasaṁghikas in the third. Thus while the Chinese evidence refers to Śaivism and Buddhism, the first two inscriptions definitely prove that Vaiṣṇavism was also introduced in the country. The second also demonstrates that the Indian philosophical ideas and religious beliefs were familiar to the people of Fu-nan. Referring to the temple of Viṣṇu, erected by Guṇavarman, it says:

"Tad-bhakto=dhivased=viśed-api ca vā tuṣṭ=āntarātmā jano |
Mukto=duṣkṛta-karmmaṇas=sa paramaṅ-gacchet padaṁ vaiṣṇavaṁ

"A devotee of Viṣṇu, who lives in, or even once enters into, this place consecrated to the god Cakratīrthasvāmī, with a contented heart, will be freed from the effects of his evil deeds, and go to the abode of Viṣṇu". The cult of *Bhakti* and the theory of *Karma* are thus clearly referred to. We are further told that the sages versed in the Śruti have given the name Cakratīrthasvāmī to the God. The name Cakratīrtha is mentioned in several Purāṇas, and a knowledge of the Puranic literature can be easily presumed from this as well as the mention of Kṣīroda-samudra and *amṛta* in the stanza of invocation. There is nothing to be surprised at this. For the record refers explicitly to Brāhmaṇas versed in Veda, Upaveda and Vedāṅga, and the first inscription mentions the houses of Brāhmaṇas in a town called Kurumbanagara.

The third inscription refers to two kings of Fu-nan named Jayavarman and his son Rudravarman. The royal eulogy is composed in the right Indian style, and the following may be cited as an example:

"Ekasthān akhilān narādhipaguṇān udyacchate vekṣitum |
Dhātrā nirmita eka eva sa bhuvi Śrī Rudravarmma...... | |

Sarvaṁ saccaritaṁ kṛtam nṛpatinā ten-āti-dharm-ārthinā |
Lokānugraha-sādhanam prati na ca kṣatravrataṁ khaṇḍitam | |

"God created Rudravarman in this world in order to collect in one place all the royal virtues. For the sake of *dharma* he, the king, performed all virtuous acts. But he did not forsake the duty of a *Kṣatriya* which contributes to the welfare of men". King Jayavarman, we are told, appointed the son of the leading Brāhmaṇa (*dvija-nāyaka*) as his treasurer (*dhanānām-adhyakṣa*). This Brāhmaṇa official adopted Buddhism and became an Upāsaka. The invocation to Buddha and the general tenor of the inscription show no trace of Mahāyāna influence whatsoever.

The records show that the caste-system, at least in its general form, was introduced in Fu-nan, although the Brāhmaṇas were by no means confined to duties of a sacerdotal character. The inscriptions, which are written in Sanskrit verse and in South Indian alphabets, show that the Sanskrit language and literature were already highly developed on the soil of Fu-nan. Although the inscriptions, particularly the last two, are fragmentary, enough remains to show that the religion and mythology of India had been carried to Cambodia and the essential elements of Hindu culture were thoroughly established in the colony of Fu-nan long before the sixth century A.D. How thoroughly Indian mythology was cultivated in Fu-nan may be illustrated by the description of Queen Kulaprabhāvatī, in the first inscription, as "Śacī is that of Śakra, Svāhā is that of Fire, Rudrāṇī that of Hara, and Śrī of Śrīpati."

Fu-nan may be regarded as one of the important centres from which Indian culture and civilisation radiated on all sides. The conquests of Fan-che-man and the establishment of an empire of Fu-nan must have facilitated the natural process by which the culture was spreading in all directions. The empire of Fu-nan must have extended over Siam, Malay Peninsula and a part of Burma, in the time of Fan-che-man. Wan-chen, a writer of the third century A.D., says that the vassal states of Fu-nan were all governed by Mandarins, and that the great officers of the right and the left of the king were called Kuen-luen. This title was borne by the king and a large number of families in Fu-nan. These must have formed the aristocracy and the ruling class, and they were the main instruments of the spread of Hindu culture and civilisation all over the empire.

The same conclusion is borne out by the study of the art of Kambuja. The monuments and sculptures of Kambuja fall readily into two broad divisions, the primitive and the classic. The latter is associated with Angkor and dates from about the 10th century. The primitive art begins from the age of Fu-nan and is continued by the early rulers of Kambuja which took its place in the 7th century A.D. As most of the monuments of the early period were made of perishable materials like wood or brick, there are not enough remains to reconstruct the art of Fu-nan. But it is now generally recognised that the primitive art of Kambuja originated during this period, and Parmentier has tried to piece together the data furnished by the primitive art in order to give some idea of the lost art of Fu-nan.[57] The temples, mostly of brick, consisted of a square or rectangular cella, with plain walls surmounted by a roof which consisted of a number of gradually receding stages. This is a characteristic of the Gupta art, and although extant specimens are wanting, we get representation of it in sculptures of the Gupta period.[58] The affinity with the Gupta art is more evident in the sculptures, and the scholars are in general agreement that the primitive art of Kambuja is derived from India and is closely allied to the Gupta art.[59] In recent years a number of sculptures have been discovered in Siam and Cambodia whose style is surprisingly akin to that of the Gupta art. Robert Dalet has described an image of Buddha found at Tuol Prah That in the district of Kompon Spur.[60] The image is broken and was found interred under the earth. The photograph shows this image to be strikingly similar in style to the Sarnath images of Buddha with which we are so familiar. This image and others of similar style found at Vat Prah Nirpan[61] leave no doubt that the primitive art of Kambuja was a direct product of the Indian school. Indeed Groslier[62] has even advanced the theory that the original Indian colonists brought with them artists and craftsmen from India, and they were entrusted with the task of building temples and images of gods. In short, whatever difference of views there might be about the origin of the classical art of Kambuja dating from 9th and 10 centuries A.D., the scholars are agreed in their view that the art of Fu-nan was purely Indian, and through Fu-nan this Indian art of the Gupta age spread over a wide territory in Indo-China along with other phases of Indian culture.

57. *BEFEO.* XXXII. pp. 183 ff.

58. For fuller discussion of this point cf. *Suvarṇadvipa*, Part II, pp. 347 ff. *History of Bengal* (Dacca University) Edited by R. C. Majumdar, pp. 493 ff.

59. cf. G Groslier—*La Sculpture Khmère Ancienne*, Ch. IX. René Grousset —*India* (Tr. by C. A. Philips) pp. 306 ff. Coedès—*Recueil des Ins. du Siam* pt. II. p. 4; *Ars Asiatica*, XII, p. 23.

60. *BEFEO.* XXXV. pp. 156 ff.

61. *Ibid*, p. 157.

62. *Op. Cit.*

LECTURE III

THE RISE OF KAMBUJADEŚA

The kingdom of Kambujadeśa, the mythical legend of whose foundation has already been mentioned above, rose into importance in the sixth century A.D. and overthrew Fu-nan. Since that time this kigndom prospered and continued its glorious existence for well-nigh seven hundred years, till the inevitable decline set in, and it was gradually reduced to a petty protectorate of the French in the 19th century A.D.

This continuity and the glory and splendour of Kambuja have cast into shade—we might almost say oblivion—the earlier kingdom of Fu-nan, with the result that the history of the Khmers now practically begins with Kambuja and their early traditions are bound up with it.

Kambuja, as noted above, was one of the many states which acknowledged the suzerainty of Fu-nan. Its early history is obscure but we may glean a few important facts from a study of the inscriptions and Chinese accounts.

The Baksei Camkron Ins. (No. 89) dated 869 Śaka (=947 A.D.), which gives the traditional account of the descent of the Kambuja kings from the great sage Kambu Svāyambhuva, refers to Śrutavarman as the root (*mūla*) of the rulers of Kambu who delivered the country from bondage (*lit.* chains of tribute). Another inscription, found at Ta Prohm (No. 177) and dated 1108 S' (=1186 A.D.), mentions king Śrutavarman and his son king Śreṣṭhavarman. The latter is described as the sun in the sky which is the family of Kambu, and is said to have been the progenitor of the royal line (*vasudhādhara-vaṁśa-yoni*). He was born on the mountain Jayādityapura and was the supreme king of Śreṣṭhapura.

We may, therefore, regard Śrutavarman and his son Śreṣṭhavarman as the earliest historical kings of Kambuja. Fortunately, the reference to Śreṣṭhapura enables us to locate the kingdom over which they ruled. An inscription (No. 170) found at Vat Phu, near Bassac in Laos, records that the locality was included in the district (*viṣaya*) of Śreṣṭhapura. It would thus appear that originally the kingdom of Kambu occupied this region to the north-east of Cambodia.[1] It is perhaps possible to locate definitely the capital of this kingdom. According to the History of the Sui dynasty the capital of Chen-la was close to a hill called Leng-kia-po-po on the summit of which there was a temple. To the east of the town lived a spirit named Po-to-li to which human sacrifice was offered. The Chinese name of the hill can easily be restored as Liṅgaparvata, which according to Ins. No. 33 (V. 4) was the ancient name of the Vat Phu Hill. The Chinese name of the spirit may be derived from the first two letters of Bhadreśvara, the presiding deity of Vat Phu. An inscription (No. 170) also refers to the country of Bhadreśvarāspada as included in the Viṣaya of Śreṣṭhapura. There can be hardly any doubt, therefore, that Śreṣṭhapura, the capital of the earliest kingdom of Kambuja, was in the immediate neighbourhood of Vat Phu.[2]

It may be legitimately inferred from what has been said above that Kambuja was civilised by the Hindu immigrants who had possibly come at different times and set up different kingdoms, all of which at first acknowledged the suzerainty of Fu-nan. Śrutavarman, the first historical king of Kambuja known to us, evidently united some of these petty states into a powerful kingdom and freed it from the yoke of Fu-nan. Śreṣṭhavarman succeeded his father Śrutavarman and ruled as a powerful king at Śreṣṭhapura near Vat Phu.

The statement in the Baksei Camkron Ins. (No. 89) that the kings of this family delivered Kambu from bondage requires further elucidation. There can be hardly any doubt that the bondage refers to the suzerainty of Fu-nan. But who delivered Kambu from the yoke of Fu-nan? He may be either Śrutavarman or Śreṣṭhavarman or one of his successors of whom nothing is known. But the independence seems to have been achieved before a new dynasty founded by Bhavavarman succeeded them in Kambuja.

The Ta Prohm Ins., referred to above, mentions this king Bhavavarman as lord of Bhavapura, and he is expressly stated to be the founder of a line of kings. This is corroborated by V. 5 of the Ang Chumnik Ins. (No. 27) which says that he got his kingdom by his own prowess (*sva-śakty-ākrānta-rājya*). His father Vīravarman is referred to in two inscriptions (Nos. 9 and 11), but there is nothing to indicate that the latter was a king. Thus evi-

1. *BEFEO.* XVIII. No. 9. pp. 1-2.
2. *BEFEO.* XXVIII. p. 124.

dence, both positive and negative, confirms the statement in the Ta-Prohm. Ins., that Bhavavarman was the founder of a new line of kings.

Important light is thrown on the history of the royal line founded by Bhavavarman by the succession of kings referred to in the Ang-Chumnik Ins. (No. 27). This inscription mentions a family of physicians and the names of kings served by them. It begins with two brothers Brahmadatta and Brahmasiṁha who were physicians of king Rudravarman. Their nephews (sister's sons) *viz.*, Dharmadeva and Siṁhadeva, were physicians respectively of kings Bhavavarman and Mahendravarman. Siṁhavīra, son of Dharmadeva, was a minister of king Īśānavarman, and lastly Siṁhadatta, son of Siṁhavīra, was the physician of king Jayavarman and governor of Ādhyapura.

The inscription thus gives a list of succession of kings as follows:

Rudravarman
Bhavavarman
Mahendravarman
Īśānavarman
Jayavarman.

This list is partly confirmed by an inscription of Prakāśadharman king of Champā dated 658 A.D. which refers to Bhavavarman, king of Kambuja, and his two immediate successors, his brother Mahendravarman and the latter's son Īśānavarman.[3] The relationship of the first two kings in the series cannot be ascertained, but Bhavavarman was certainly not the son of Rudravarman, for his father's name, as noted above, was Vīravarman.

Mahendravarman, according to the Ins. No. 11, was the son of Śrī-Vīravarman and the younger brother of Bhavavarman. The same inscription tells us that his original name was Citrasena, but he assumed the name Mahendravarman at the time of his coronation.

The name Citrasena is known to us from the Chinese texts. The History of the Sui Dynasty (589-618) gives the following account of Chen-la.[4]

3. *Champa*, Bk. III. pp. 18-19, 23-24.

4. The account given in the History of the Sui dynasty is translated by M. Abel Remusat in Nouveaux Melanges Asiatique, Vol. I, pp. 77 ff. (Paris 1829). It refers to the period 589-618 A.D. All subsequent references to Chinese Chronicles, unless otherwise stated, are from this work,

"It is situated to the south-west of Lin-yi (Champa). It was originally a vassal state of Fu-nan. The family name of the king was Kṣatriya. His personal name was Citrasena. His ancestors had gradually increased the power of the kingdom. Citrasena made himself master of Fu-nan. He died. His son Īśānasena succeeded him. He inhabited the town of Īśāna". The same text adds that the first embassy from Chen-la came in 616 or 617 A.D. and it was obviously sent by Īśānasena.

Another Chinese text Nan–che tells us that the king Kṣatriya Īśāna, at the beginning of the period Cheng-kuan (627–649 A.D.), conquered Fu–nan and took possession of the kingdom.[5]

The discrepancy in the Chinese texts, one attributing the conquest of Fu–nan to Citrasena and the other to his son Īśāna, may perhaps be best reconciled by supposing that the conquest of Fu-nan was a gradual process. The struggle with Fu-nan must have commenced even before the reign of Citrasena, for the History of the Sui Dynasty states that the power of the kingdom of Chen-la was increased by his ancestors. The only reasonable and natural inference from all these is that Bhavavarman began to aggrandise the kingdom of Kambuja at the expense of Fu-nan, and his two successors, *viz.*, his brother Citrasena or Mahendravarman and the latter's son Īśānasena or Īśānavarman, completed the conquest of the country. It is probable that Citrasena conquered the northern part of the state, but the capital of Fu–nan was occupied, and that kingdom was finally conquered, by the last named king.[6]

It is not difficult now to identify Rudravarman, the first king and predecessor of Bhavavarman in the succession list furnished by the Ang Chumnik Inscription. As we have seen above, Rudravarman is the name of the last king of Fu–nan mentioned in the Chinese chronicles, and his last known date is 539 A.D. As Bhavavarman was removed by one generation from his predecessor Rudravarman, and as Īśānavarman, the son of his brother, was on the throne before 617 A.D., there can be hardly any doubt that king Rudravarman, served by the two physicians Brahmadatta and Brahmasimha, as mentioned in the Ang Chumnik Ins., was the king of Fu-nan of that name.

5. *BEFEO*. III, p. 275.

6. This has been treated with fuller details in Lecture II. Cf. also *BEFEO* XXVIII. 130

Thus on the basis of the epigraphic and Chinese data we may reconstruct the history of the dynasty of Bhavavarman somewhat as follows:

Some time about the middle of the sixth century A.D. Bhavavarman acquired the throne of Kambuja and considerably increased its power and extent. His brother Mahendravarman, who succeeded him, led many military expeditions against Rudravarman, the king of Fu-nan. He succeeded in conquering nearly the whole of the kingdom and probably even seized its capital. Rudravarman, or his successor who was then on the throne of Fu-nan, fled to the south and his dynasty continued to rule over a petty state in the extreme south of Cambodia with a new capital city. But the struggle between the two powers continued during the reign of Īśānavarman, the son and successor of Mahendravarman. Īśānavarman finally extinguished the kingdom of Fu-nan, probably about 630 A.D.

Having thus definitely laid down, in outline, the course of events by which the vassal state of Kambuja came to take the place of the old kingdom of Fu-nan, we may now proceed to discuss its history in some details.

It is evident that there were two separate royal dynasties—one founded by Śrutavarman, and the other by Bhavavarman. The first dynasty at first acknowledged the suzerainty of Fu-nan, but seems later to have achieved the independence of the kingdom. But it was under the second dynasty that Kambuja became great and powerful and ultimately took the place of Fu-nan as suzerain of the whole of Cambodia.

Of the two kings Śrutavarman and Śreṣṭhavarman of the first dynasty we know but little. Nor do we know how they were connected with Bhavavarman who was the real founder of the second dynasty. That there was some connection may be presumed from the qualifying expression '*Śrutavarma-mūla*' applied to the kings of Kambuja. This general reference to Śrutavarman, as the common ancestor of the Kambuja kings, is corroborated by the fact that even king Jayavarman VII, who ruled towards the close of the twelfth century A.D., claims to have been descended from Śreṣthavarman, the supreme king of Śreṣthapura (No. 177, vv. 6-7). King Udayādityavarman I is also said to have been descended through his mother from the family of Śreṣṭhapura (No. 117 v. 5).

The Ta Prohm Ins. (No. 177) seems to throw some light on the relation between the two dynasties. After referring to Śreṣṭhavarman in v. 7 it devotes the next verse to the eulogy of a lady, born in his maternal family (*tadīye mātṛ-kul-āmburāśau*). She is called Kambuja-rāja-lakṣmī. This has been taken as a proper name-but must be regarded as a very unusual one. It may be also taken as a descriptiye epithet, though in that case we have to assume that the personal name of the lady is not mentioned. The next verse, *i.e.*, v. 9, refers to Bhavavarman as '*bhartā bhuvo Bhavapure*' and '*avanīndra-kula-prasūteḥ karttā*'. These two expressions may mean no more than that Bhavavarman was the lord of Bhavapura and the founder of a royal family, but may also contain a veiled allusion to the fact that he was the husband of the lady. If some relationship did not subsist between Bhavavarman and this lady, it is difficult to account for the insertion of v. 8 between the eulogy of Śreṣṭhavarman in v. 7 and that of Bhavavarman in v. 9. If there was any relationship, the expressions referred to above would certainly favour the hypothesis that Bhavavarman was the husband of this lady.

This hypothesis is supported by another consideration. The Ta Prohm Ins. (No. 177) compares Śreṣṭhavarman to the sun and Bhavavarman to the moon, while the Baksei Camkron Ins. (No. 89) claims that the lineage of Kambu Svāyambhuva brought about the alliance of the solar and lunar races. A consideration of all the facts leads to a reasonable inference that the families of Śrutavarman and Bhavavarman were connected by marriage, even though we may not regard Bhavavarman as the husband of the lady called Kambuja-rāja-lakṣmī.

The original kingdom of Kambuja must, as noted above, have comprised the region of Bassac along the river Mekong where it emerges from Laos into Cambodia proper, the capital city, Śreṣṭhapura, being situated near the modern sanctuary of Vat Phu. This was the early seat of the Kambuja rulers traditionally associated with Kambu Svāyambhuva. With Bhavavarman, there is not only a change of capital city to Bhavapura, but also a break in that tradition. Bhavavarman, Mahendravarman and their successors make no allusion either to Kambu or to Śreṣṭhapura, but describe themselves, like kings of Fu-nan, as descendants of Kauṇḍinya and Somā. It has been suggested[7] that this was a clever political move on their part in order to make themselves appear as the legitimate heirs of the kings of Fu-nan. Perhaps the same motive also impelled them to build numerous religious sanctuaries in the southern

7. *BEFEO*. XVIII. No. 9. p. 3.

regions. In any case it was not till the reign of Jayavarman II in the ninth century A.D. that the kings of Kambuja again refer to the old tradition of Kambu, Śreṣṭhapura, Sūryavaṁśa etc. As by that time the glory of Fu-nan was a thing of the remote past, and the political centre of Kambuja was shifted far to the north, it was perhaps no longer necessary to recall its traditions.

This explanation is no doubt a plausible one, but does not carry immediate conviction. It is equally possible that Bhavavarman was more intimately connected with the kings of Fu-nan than we yet know, and that may be the reason why he and his successors carried on the old traditions of that kingdom. As noted above, he founded a new kingdom. Several records refer to his grandfather as '*sārvabhauma*' i.e., a suzerain or emperor, but there is no evidence that his father Vīravarman was ever a reigning king. It has been suggested, with some degree of plausibility, that the suzerain was no other than Rudravarman, king of Fu-nan, whose name heads the list of kings in the Ang Chumnik Ins. referred to above. According to this theory the death of Rudravarman was followed by a disputed succession between two princes, one living at Fu-nan, and the other, Bhavavarman, who got the kingdom of Kambuja as his appanage. Ultimately Bhavavarman got the better of his rival, and his successors finally extinguished the main line of kings at Fu-nan and ruled over the whole country. This theory[8] no doubt lacks definite proof, but certainly offers an explanation of the change of traditions which is hardly less plausible than the one mentioned above. It also offers a better explanation of v. 16 of Ins. No. 89 which refers to 'kings beginning with Rudravarman' as succeeding the royal line of Śrutavarman.

Without pursuing any further the speculative hypothesis regarding the relation of Bhavavarman with the dynasty of Śrutavarman of Kambuja on the one hand and the royal family of Fu-nan on the other, we may now proceed to reconstruct his history on the basis of epigraphic evidence. As regards his ancestry, it has been incidentally mentioned above that he was the son of Vīravarman and the grandson of Sārvabhauma. This we know from six records (No. 11) which are nearly identical, and commence with the following verse about Mahendravarman.

> ***Naptā śrī-Sārvabhaumasya sūnus=śrī-Vīravarmaṇah |***
> ***Saktyā=nūno kaniṣṭho =pi bhrātā śrī-Bhavavarmaṇaḥ ||***

8. *BEFEO.* XXVIII, pp. 130-31. *Melange Sylvain Lévi*, pp. 210-11; *BCAI*, 1911, p. 36.

It means that Mahendravarman was the grandson of Śrī-Sārva-bhauma, the son of Vīravarman, and the youngest brother of Bhavavarman, although not inferior to the last in prowess. That Bhavavarman was the son of Vīravarman is also known from Ins. No. 9 which refers to the wife of the donor as a daughter of Vīravarman and sister of Bhavavarman. It is worthy of remark that in both the cases Vīravarman is mentioned without any royal title. This raises some doubts about the view, mentioned above, which seeks to interpret the word Śrī Sārvabhauma as suzerain instead of taking it as a personal name of his grandfather. The prefix Śrī seems to indicate it as a personal name,[9] and the context in which it occurs is undoubtedly in favour of this interpretation. On the other hand it must be admitted that this is rather an unusual name for a person (though names like Ācārya Vidyā-Vinaya (No. 22) are not less so), and the absence of a name-ending like Varman is also against this view. On the whole the question must be left open.

The history of Bhavavarman's reign has been usually reconstructed on the basis of Inscriptions Nos. 5-9 all of which mention king Bhavavarman but do not contain any date. As no other king of this name was known until the discovery of Ins. No. 24, all the five inscriptions were referred to Bhavavarman, the founder of this dynasty, and very important conclusions were drawn from them about his life and reign. As usually happens, these have not been seriously questioned even after the discovery of the Ins. No. 24 which definitely establishes the existence of a second king of that name who flourished more than a century after his namesake. Thus it is generally concluded from the findspots of these five inscriptions that Bhavavarman was a great conqueror and extended his kingdom up to the province of Battambang in the west (No. 7). This would mean that he was master of nearly the whole of Cambodia with the possible exception of a small strip of territory to the south. This is hardly consistent with the Chinese account which attributes to Mahendravarman and his son the conquest of the kingdom of Fu-nan which comprised at least a large part of these territories, if not the whole of them. It is no doubt possible to reconcile the Chinese account with the epigraphic data by arguing that Bhavavarman conquered all the outlying possessions of Fu–nan leaving to his successors the task of finally subjugating the small kingdom

9. Coedès also holds this view (*BEFEO*, XXII. 58-59).

of Fu-nan proper. But the fact remains that we have no right to assume that Bhavavarman I really exercised sovereignty over such a vast area. For some of the inscriptions at any rate might belong to the reign of Bhavavarman II. As a matter of fact Ins. No. 9 alone can be definitely assigned to the reign of Bhavavarman I, from the mention of his father's name, but the remaining four might belong to the reign of either of the two kings bearing the name Bhavavarman. Palaeography is not of much help in distinguishing the records of the two kings, for as Coedès has rightly pointed out, the essential features of the Kambuja alphabet remained unaltered up to the time of Jayavarman I. Nevertheless he has suggested from certain characteristics in the style of writing that the Ins. Nos. 7 and 8 should be attributed to Bhavavarman II,[10] and even this would take away the evidence for the southern limit of the kingdom of Bhavavarman I, referred to above. All that, therefore, we can definitely say is that Bhavavarman ruled in the north-eastern part of Cambodia where Ins. No. 9 was found. The inscriptions Nos. 5, 6, 8 describe the virtues and prowess of the king in the most extravagant manner and in a high-flown *kāvya* style in right Indian fashion. But beyond denoting the limits of the kingdom they yield very little historical information. The Han Chey Ins. (No. 8) gives him the title Mahārājādhirāja and says that he has violated the honour of the Aila race only inasmuch as he has, by his prowess, exceeded the limits of their territories (v. A. 17). It refers to his conquest of hill-forts (v. B. 5) and adds that 'enemies, although not vanquished in battle, are attracted by his influence and bow down at his lotus feet with the offer of princely fortune' (v. A. 13). But as already noted above, it is doubtful whether the Han Chey Ins. is to be attributed to Bhavavarman I or Bhavavarman II.

There is some uncertainty about the successor of Bhavavarman I. The Chinese evidence, and other epigraphic records, noted above, seem to suggest that Bhavavarman was succeeded by his brother Citrasena. On the other hand the Han Chey Ins. (No. 8) definitely asserts that the younger son of Bhavavarman peacefully ascended the throne of his father, and the donor mentioned in that record is said to have served under both these kings (v. 22). This Bhavavarman has been taken to be Bhavavarman I, although, as noted above, the identity cannot be regarded as certain. But if we accept

10. *BEFEO*. IV, p. 694.

the identity we must hold that Bhavavarman's son had a short reign. It is impossible to say in that case whether he had a natural death at a young age or was killed by his uncle Citrasena. That such a contingency was not very unlikely is proved by the following observation in a Chinese account which was recorded not very long after the accession of Citrasena: "The day a new king ascends the throne his brothers are mutilated by their nose or fingers being cut, and they are kept in confinement, each in a separate place".

Citrasena—Mahendravarman has left us two records. The first of these (No. 10) under the former name has three copies at Cruoy Anphil, Thma kre, and Tham Pet Thong. The second (No. 11) under the latter name is known from six copies (more or less exact) at Chan Nakhon (Phu Bahkon), Khan Thevada (2 copies), Tham Prasat, Muang Surin, and near Keng Tana. It is expressly stated in the second that he was formerly known as Citrasena and assumed the name Mahendravarman at the time of coronation. It may therefore be argued that the first series of records were engraved before he ascended the throne, particularly as no royal epithet is given to him. But it must be pointed out that the Chinese call him Citrasena even after he became king. It may also be doubted if the findspots of these inscriptions were included within the kingdom. But it is certainly more reasonable to hold that they were, and on that hypothesis we may regard the kingdom of Kambuja as having been extended in the south along the Mekong valley up to Thma Kre beyond Sambor, and in the west along the Mun valley up to Tham Pet Thong near the sources of that river in Rajasima district in Siam beyond the Dangrek mountains. Whether these territories were conquered by Citrasena or his predecessors must be left an open question. The inscriptions of Mahendravarman show a further extension of his kingdom to the north along the valley of the Mekong up to the region of Chan Nakhon beyond Basac. But none of his inscriptions has been found to the west of M. Surin which lies considerably to the east of Tham Pet Thong. The Chinese accounts referred to above would indicate that he proceeded further south along the Mekong valley towards Fu-nan, and conquered the capital of that kingdom situated probably at Ba Phnom, but it is difficult to fix the limits of his conquest.

The Chinese accounts also enable us to fix the date of Mahendravarman within narrow limits. His conquest of Fu-nan, his death, and the accession of Īśānavarman must all be placed during 589 to 618 A.D., the period covered by the History of the Sui dynasty which refers to them. The same chronicle refers to an embassy from Kambuja in the year 616 or 617 A.D.[11] As the Chinese account was presumably based upon the report of this embassy, it must have been sent by Īśānavarman. Mahendravarman, therefore, must have died before 616 or 617 A.D. As Rudravarman, the last known king of Fu-nan, certainly ruled from 517 to 539 A.D. and Bhavavarman was removed by only one generation from him, the date of the two brothers Bhavavarman and Mahendravarman may be roughly placed between 550 and 600 A.D.

The Ang Chumnik Ins. (No. 27) tells us that Mahendravarman sent an ambassador to the king of Champā for renewing the friendship between the two nations. It may be concluded, in the light of later events, that Kambuja had deliberately begun to play a part in the politics of that neighbouring kingdom which bore such important results in the next reign.

Īśānavarman succeeded his father Mahendravarman about 600 A.D. According to a Chinese text Īśānavarman put his brothers in solitary confinement in order to put an end to the rivalry for the throne.[12] The main event of his reign was the protracted struggle with Fu-nan, for as noted above, Mahendravarman, in spite of his successes could not finally subjugate the country, and its king, though forced to remove his capital further south, still maintained a precarious existence in a corner of his kingdom. He, however, evidently offered stubborn resistance as it was not till 627 A.D., and possibly a few years later, that Īśānavarman finally extinguished the kingdom and took possession of its territory.[13] The Chinese account is corroborated by the inscriptions of the king as they are found in the valley of the lower Mekong, both to the east and west of Chaudoc (Nos. 12 and 18). There is no doubt that his kingdom extended along the valley of the Mekong from its junction with the Mun to its mouth. His kingdom must have comprised the whole of Cambodia and also the valley of the Mun to the north of the Dangrek mountains. The Vat Chakret Ins.

11. *BEFEO*. III, p. 272.

12. E. Aymonier—*Histoire de l'Ancien Cambodge*, p. 32. I have not been able to verify this statement. It seems to be based merely on the general observation, referred to above, in the History of the Sui Dynasty, which naturally may be taken as applicable to the case of Īśānavarman whose embassy to China supplied the requisite information to the Chinese historian.

13. According to the *New History of the T'ang Dynasty* Īśānavarman conquered Fu-nan at the beginning of the period 627-649. The same text refers to an embassy from Fu-nan during the same period (*BEFEO*. III, pp. 274-75).

(No. 21) dated in the year 549 Śaka or 627 A.D. says that he, the lord of Tāmrapura, possessed the three cities of Cakrāṅkapura, Amoghapura, and Bhīmapura. Of these the first has been identified with Chikreng or Chakreng to the south-east of Angkor, the second with Battambang, and the third with Phimai on the Semun.[14] An inscription found near Chantabun shows that the region on the border of Siam was included within the domains of Īśānavarman.[15] The epigraphic evidence supports the statement of Hiuen Tsang that Īśānavarman's kingdom comprised the central part of Indo-China, with the kingdom of Dvāravatī (Central Siam) on the west and Mahā-Champā (Annam) on the east.[16]

Īśānavarman transferred his capital to a city named after him Īśānapura. This has been identified with Sambor Prei Kuk,[17] where a large number of his inscriptions have been found. This was the beginning of that shifting of the seat of political authority towards the west which ultimately led to the establishment of the political centre of Kambuja in the Angkor region.

As already noted above, Īśānavarman sent an embassy to China in 616 or 617 A.D. Īśānavarman's name is also intimately associated with the history of Champā. That kingdom was then passing through a series of palace revolutions and political intrigues of which the exact nature is difficult to determine. It is quite clear that the kings of Kambuja, specially Mahendravarman and his son, took an active part in its affairs. The daughter of Īśānavarman, princess Śrī Sarvāṇī, was married to Jagaddharma of Champā, and ultimately her son Prakāśadharma secured the throne of Champā and restored order and tranquility.[18]

The list of kings preserved in the Ang Chumnik Ins. gives the name of Jayavarman after that of Īśānavarman. The Ins. No. 24, however, reveals the existence of a king Bhavavarman reigning in 561 Śaka or 639 A.D. As Īśānavarman was on the throne in 627

14. Maspero—*L'Empire Khmer*, p. 27 fn. *BEFEO*. XXIV, pp. 359 ff.

15. BEFEO. XXIV. pp. 352-358. It was held by Lajonquierre that the Khmers did not extend their power to the Chantabun region till the 9th century A.D. But a fragmentary inscription at Chantabun containing the name of Īśānavarman, and another at Khalung, in the same region, disprove this view.

16. Beal—*Records*, II. p. 200.

17. *BEFEO*. XXVIII, p. 125.

18. *Champa*—pp. 39-45.

A.D. (No. 20) and the earliest known date of Jayavarman is 657 A.D., the reign of Bhavavarman II may be placed between 635 and 650 A.D. Unfortunately we know nothing of this king, not even his relationship with the two kings mentioned above. An inscription (No. 23) at Phnom Bayan mentions a donation by king Bhavavarman to Utpanneśvara (probably a form of Śiva). This Bhavavarman has been identified with Bhavavarman II. The inscription contains a reference to Kauṇḍinya and his queen at the beginning and mentions the 'descendants of the lunar race of....Śrī Koṇgavarman'. This latter name is otherwise unknown in the history of Kambuja, but recalls the similar names of the Gaṅga kings of India.[19]

The next king known to us, Jayavarman I, is referred to in several inscriptions (Nos. 22, 25–27, 30, 30A, 32, 33, 34) which refer, in general terms, to his great prowess and conquests and manifold virtues. His relationship with the preceding kings is not known. The earliest known date of his reign is 657 A.D. (No. 25) and the latest 674 A.D. (Ins. No. 30A). Ins. No. 26 refers to the transmission of certain properties by two Buddhist monks to the son of the daughter of their sister. For a long time it was believed to have been the earliest Buddhist inscription, but this has been proved to be wrong by the discovery of the Buddhist inscription of Rudravarman, the king of Fu-nan. The Ang Chumnik inscription dated 667 A.D. (No. 27), which has been frequently referred to in the preceding pages and of which a summary has been given above, was a record set up by Siṁhadatta who was at first the royal physician, and then appointed the governor of Āḍhyapura by king Jayavarman I. Jayavarman I is the last of the five or six kings who are known so far to have ruled over the kingdom founded by Bhavavarman I. The period covered by their reigns is about a century. But it may be regarded as one of the most important for the history and culture of the Hindu colonial kingdom of Kambuja.

In the case of Fu-nan we are chiefly dependent on the Chinese accounts, but as regards Kambuja, we have, in addition, the evidence of Inscriptions which throw a flood of light on the history and civilisation of the country. About one hundred inscriptions, belonging to this period are so far known to us, written both in Sanskrit and the native language Khmer. We shall now try with the help of these two-fold sources of information to reconstruct a

19. Cf. *JGIS.* V. 156.

picture of the Hindu colony of Kambuja in the seventh century A.D.

We have seen how under a line of able rulers the small vassal state of Kambuja rapidly grew to be a powerful kingdom. It not only established its authority over the whole of Cambodia and Cochin-China, but a considerable portion of modern Siam was comprised in it. The whole of the valley of the Mun river to the north of the Dangrek mountains was ruled by the Kambuja kings, and an imaginary line drawn due north from Chantabun to the source of that river represents the western limit of their kingdom as testified to by the find-spots of inscriptions and testimony of Hiuen Tsang. Part of these territories was, as it still is, inhabited by primitive savage tribes, and rendered difficult of access on account of hills and dense forest. We get a reference to it in Ins. No. 32 which records the career of an officer under king Jayavarman. This officer was appointed first as Mahāśvapati, Master of the Horse, and then as governor of Śreṣṭhapura (near Bassac in Laos) and Dhruvapura. We are told that he kept Dhruvapura free from troubles, although it was full of dense terrible forest (*bhīṣaṇ-āraṇya-saṅkaṭam*) and peopled by ferocious tribes (*uddṛpta-puruṣ-āvāsa*). Reference is also made to the defeat inflicted upon mountain chiefs (*parvata-bhūpāla*) in Ins. No. 8.

These instances[20] serve to show how, starting from the Mekong valley as the centre, the Hindu rulers of Kambuja gradually extended their power and authority towards the inaccessible regions in the north and west and gradually brought them within the sphere of Hindu culture and civilisation.

The Hindu colonists in Kambuja set up an administrative system on Indian model. The study of Arthaśāstra is specially mentioned in an inscription (No. 27, v. 6) and most probably Kautilya's Arthaśāstra or some text of this type was actually followed in practice. An interesting evidence of this is supplied by a passing reference in Ins. No. 8. The last verse of this inscription says about the donor, a royal official, that he was a favourite

20. V. 7 of the Ins. No. 7 also refers to dense forest frequented by tigers, evidently in reference to a territory conquered by Bhavavarman, but as the second line of the verse is missing, no complete sense can be made of the verse.

of the king (*antaraṅgatvam-āsthitaḥ*) as he was *sarvopadhā-śuddha*. Barth, who edited this inscription, failed to realise its meaning and recognise its importance. The term is, however, used in Kauṭilya's Arthaśāstra (I. 10) in connection with the testing of the conduct of royal officials by four kinds of allurements, which are technically known as *upadhās*. One who does not fall a prey to any of these allurements, to which he is tempted by royal spies, and thereby successfully passes all the tests, is known as *sarvo-padhāśuddha*, and Kauṭliya recommends that he should be appointed a minister. The occurrence of this word in connection with a royal servant therefore indicates that probably the method recommended by Kauṭilya was followed by Kambuja kings in the appointment of ministers.

Unfortunately the inscriptions do not enable us to form a clear idea of the system of administration as a whole, and only give us a few glimpses of it. The king's authority was supreme and a divine origin was claimed for him (No. 32, v. 3). The mention of an officer called *Rājasabhādhipati* (No. 30, v. 6) indicates the existence of a royal assembly, but we have no knowledge of its nature and constitution. The 'minister' is also frequently referred to and held an important position in state. Several high officials are mentioned in the inscriptions, but it is not always easy to distinguish their exact status and nature of duties. The *dūta* or ambassador is referred to in one record. Another high officer seems to have been something like the Chief of the royal household who was in charge of the royal insignia, particularly the valuable ornaments of the king (No. 32 v. 18). The royal physician was an important personage as Ins. 27 shows.

Several military offices are referred to. The Mahāśvapati, as the name indicates, was probably the commander of cavalry. Another highly honourable post was that of the leader of the royal body-guard (*nṛp-āntaraṅga-yaudha*) composed of soldiers with arms and helmets. It is perhaps this body which is referred to in the following passage in a Chinese Chronicle: "In front of the chamber containing the royal throne there are thousand guards armed with cuirass and lances". Two naval officers are mentioned, *mahā-nauvāhaka* (No. 45) and *Samanta-nauvāha* (No. 32, v. 18). The latter is said to be the head of the boatmen (*Taritra-bhṛt*) who knows their classification.

The inscriptions frequently refer to war elephants. According to a statement in the History of the Tang dynasty which appears from the context to refer to the 7th century A.D., there were five thousand war-elephants in Kambuja.

There seem to be different gradations of military rank. The commander of a body of troops living in a single city is called *Sahasra-Vargg-ādhipatiḥ* (No. 32, v. 19). The word '*vargga*' evidently stands for a unit, and the title probably means the commander of a unit of thousand soldiers, rather than one of thousand units.

The kingdom was divided into a large number of districts each with a governor living in a city as his headquarter. The same Chinese chronicle tells us that there were thirty towns with several thousands of houses in each, and every town had a governor. Evidently the kingdom was divided into thirty administrative units, each with a headquarter at a city. The inscriptions not only confirm this but supply us with names of a number of such towns viz. Pasenga (?), Tatandarapura, Tāmrapura, Āḍhyapura, Śreṣṭhapura, Bhavapura, Dhruvapura, Dhanvipura, Jyeṣṭhapura, Vikramapura, Ugrapura, and Īśānapura.

The towns were surrounded by walls and ditches. Among the amenities of life provided therein are mentioned public institutions like *Vipraśālā, Sarasvatī* (Public school or library?), *satra* (guest house or hospital), and tanks, both big and small (No. 32, v. 8), *bhaktaśālā* (alms-house) and a *śilāvandhana* (bridge ?) (No. 46).

A pointed reference to Īśānavarman as suzerain of three kings and lord of three cities perhaps indicates that there were three vassal states (No. 19) not directly administered by royal officials but enjoying some sort of internal autonomy. These three cities were probably Cakrāṅkapura, Amoghapura and Bhīmapura (No. 21) mentioned above.

As in ancient India the posts of minister and other high officials were often hereditary, the most notable being the case recorded in Ins. No. 27 to which reference has been made above. The governors, ministers and other high officials received marks of distinction from the sovereign by the gift of a golden car and umbrella with golden embroidery, golden vessels (*karaṅka-kalasa*), horses, elephants, retinue, etc.

The court of Kambuja, which may be said to have developed into an empire, introduced pomp and grandeur befitting its power and glory. The contemporary Chinese chronicles[21] give a very interesting account of the court and capital of Īśānavarman which is quoted below.

"After Citrasena's death his son Yi-che-na-sian-tai (Īśānasena or Īśānavarman) succeeded him. He lived in a town named Yi-chen-na (Īśānapura). This town contained 20,000 houses. At the centre was a grand palace where the king held his court. Three days a week, the king sits in the court, on a seat decorated with five kinds of aromatics and seven kinds of precious stones. A costly canopy like a pavilion is placed over his head. Its columns are of painted wood. The walls are decorated with ivory and flowers of gold. The pavilion looks like a small hanging palace, all shining with gold. Two bowls of gold with the aromatics are carried by two men on two sides of the king. His crown is decorated with pearls and precious stones. His shoes are made of skin of different colours and decorated with ivory. He wears golden ear-rings and is always dressed in white. There are five kinds of high officers and they are dressed like the king. The officers touch the ground three times in front of the throne of the king. The king then commands them to ascend the stairs and having done so they kneel down before the king with folded hands. They are then seated in a circle round the king for discussing state affairs. When the deliberation is over they kneel down, again prostrate themselves and go out.

In contrast to the meagre information about administrative system, we possess a fair knowledge about the religion of Kambuja. Most of the inscriptions begin with an invocation to one or more gods and record donations to religious establishments. Taken as a whole they clearly indicate the strong hold of Indian religion on the population. Although Vedic sacrifices are referred to (Nos. 19, 20), the Puranic form of religion, specially the worship of Śiva, Viṣṇu and the deities associated with them, was undoubtedly more predominant. The most popular god seems to be Śiva though the composite deity Śiva-Viṣṇu, designated as Śaṅkara-Nārāyaṇa, Śambhu-Viṣṇu (*liṅga*), Har-āchyuta, Hari-Śaṅkara etc., was also in great favour. Śiva is occasionally referred to as the greatest god, whose feet are worshipped by Brhamā and Viṣṇu. He is described as a great ascetic and is known by various names

21. *History of the Sui Dynasty*—see f.n. 4 above.

such as Āmrātakeśvara, Rudra, Vyomeśvara, Gambhīreśvara, Nikāmeśvara, Piṅgaleśvara, Naimiseśvara, Īśāna, Śrīvijayeśvara, Kedāreśvara, Giriśa, Śambhu, Tryambaka, Siddheśa, Triśūlī, Śaṅkara, Tribhuvaneśvara, Nṛtteśvara, Acaleśvara, Kadambeśvara, Maheśvara, Utpanneśvara or Uppannakeśvara, and was mostly worshipped in his *liṅga*-form. He bore Ganges on the forehead and had moon as his crest jewel. His Bull (Nandin) was also regarded as sacred. The goddesses of the Hindu pantheon are not unknown and we have references to Umā, Durgā Devīcaturbhujā, Bhagavatī, Lakṣmī and Sarasvatī. Of the various names and forms of Viṣṇu we come across Trailokyasāra, Hari, Acyuta and Nārāyaṇa. Reference is also made to Śālagrāma in a record by engraving a figure of it after the name of the donor Śālagrāmasvāmī.

Among other deities may be mentioned Yama, Prahanteśvara, Cāndrāyananātha, Tilakeśvara, Mūlasthāna, Yajñapatīśvara, Gaṇapati and Svayambhu (Brahmā). Some of these may be names of Śiva or Viṣṇu. Buddhism was also prevalent, though judging by the number of records its influence does not seem to have been very great. According to the Chinese chronicle, however, there were many followers of Buddhism. One inscription refers to three Bodhisatvas, Śāstā, Maitreya and Avalokiteśvara. The epigraphic evidence is corroborated by the cult images actually discovered in Cambodia, among which mention may be made of Hari-Hara, Śiva, Pārvatī, Nandin (Bull of Śiva), Brahmā and Buddha. The images of the deities were placed in temples ruins of which lie scattered all over the country. The temple, near the capital, on the top of a hill, enjoyed special sanctity, and according to Chinese chronicle was guarded by five thousand soldiers. As in India, kings, high officials and even private persons vied with one another in setting up divine images, building temples for them and making endowments for the regular performance of their worship. The endowments generally consisted of gold, village, land (paddy fields), orchard, servants (both male and female, generally slaves), beautiful women, probably *devadāsīs* (No. 32, v. 22), cattle (cow, buffalo), arecanut and cocoanut trees. There were festivals of citizens in honour of Śiva (No. 22). Frequent reference is made to *āśramas* and we find already in the seventh century A.D. the beginning of those regulations which, multiplied and codified at a later age, form such a distinctive characteristic of Kambuja sanctuaries. It was, for example, laid down in an edict of Jayavarman (No. 33) regarding the temple on Liṅgaparvata (Vat Phu) that no one living there, even if guilty, should be killed, that no one should go wherever he likes in this *āśrama* of god, use a car, an umbrella or a flywhisk, or bring dogs and fowls.

The study of sacred literature is referred to in many inscriptions and we hear of Brāhmaṇas proficient in Veda, Vedāṅga, Sāmaveda, and Buddhist scriptures, and even ministers with a profound knowledge of Dharmaśāstra.

Reference is made to the daily recitation of the Rāmāyaṇa, the Mahābhārata and the Purāṇas (No. 9). The inscriptions reveal a thorough acquaintance of their authors with these works. Ins. No. 36 refers to the gift of a manuscript of Sambhava, a work of Vyāsa. There is no doubt that it refers to the section of Ādiparva of Mahābhārata, called Sambhavaparva. Imprecations are invoked against anybody who destroys the manuscript deposited in the temple.

Some of the invocations to God indicate that along with popular forms of worship religious philosophy of India was cultivated to a high degree. Reference is made to the attainment of '*Brahmapada*' or *Niruttara Brahma* as spiritual goal of life. Prominence is given to the all-pervading character of Śiva whose eight bodies (*aṣṭa tanu*) consist of the moon, sun, sky, air, the *ātman*, earth, water and fire. The invocation to Śiva in Ins. No. 4 illustrates Vedantic Śaivism in which Śiva is identified with *Paramātman*, or the *Absolute* of the Upanishads. The spiritual doctrine of the cessation of desire for the fruit of *karma* (action) as laid down in the Bhagavadgītā is also echoed in it.

A short record *Oṁ Jaiminaye svāhā*,[22] shows the great reverence for Pūrva-Mīmāṁsā, and probably indicates that its author was regarded as a deity and regularly worshipped.

Some peculiar religious ideas of India are also met with. It is said of a royal official that he gratified the gods by Śivayajña, the ascetics by study, and the manes by the water offered by good sons (No. 27, v. 23). Reference is also made to *tīrthas* (holy places) and merits of pilgrimage. The Śaiva Pāśupata sect evidently wielded great influence, and an inscription refers to its *ācārya* Vidyāpuṣpa as a poet and versed in various branches of philosophy (No. 6).

22. *BEFEO*. XXVIII, p. 43.

Some debased forms of Śaiva religion were also prevalent. According to the Chinese chronicle there was a temple to the east of the capital city, guarded by thousand soldiers, where the king went every year to sacrifice a human being. The Purāṇic myths and legends were also very familiar and the inscriptions abound in allusions to them. There are references to the churning of the ocean; the Kailāsa; the Udayagiri; Kārtika as general of the gods; *dharma* crippled in Kaliyuga; the burning of the cupid; sacred character of *tīrthas* (including hills); lunar and solar races; Arundhatī, the ideal wife; Śeṣanāga, supporting the earth; Indra, the wielder of thunderbolt, and with thousand eyes, clipping the wings of mountains and performing hundred sacrifices (No. 20); Manu the first king; Dilīpa as an ideal king; Aśvinī as the divine physician etc., etc.

The secular literature was also regularly studied, and the inscriptions refer to many of its branches such as Śabda, Vaiśeṣika, Nyāya, Samīkṣa (Sāṅkhya?) and Arthaśāstra. The Kāvya formed a favourite subject of study, and even a minister is described (No. 27) as having drunk the nectar of poetry (*āpīta-kavitā-rasaḥ*).

The Śaka era was exclusively used and the expressions denoting date show a thorough acquaintance with the astronomical system of India. Reference is made to a governor, proficient in astrology (*bhojakapravara*—No. 20).

The inscriptions themselves furnish the best testimony to the assiduous cultivation of Sanskrit language and literature in Kambuja. Many of them are fairly long poems written in rich *kāvya* style and show high proficiency in the knowledge of Sanskrit grammar, vocabulary, idiom, rhetoric, prosody, metre and poetic conventions and styles. That the classical works in Sanskrit were regularly studied is evident from the use of familiar similes, comparisons and allegories in the inscriptions, and it would be difficult to distinguish them from the *praśastis* composed in India. Judged by any standard, the writings of the Kambuja scholars must be regarded as no mean contribution to Sanskrit literature.

As regards society, Indian institutions exercised great influence but were partially modified by indigenous ideas and customs. Of the caste divisions we find mention only of Brāhmaṇas and Kṣatriyas. Reference is made to Brāhmaṇas who were proficient in Veda and Vedāṅgas and whose family for generations served as *hotars* (sacrificial priests). But even members of this family, as also of others, served in various offices of state, both civil and military. There thus seems to have been no rigidity of caste-rule as regards occupation. Inter-marriage between Brāhmaṇa and Kṣatriya seems to have been a normal custom. The sister of king Bhavavarman, for example, was married to a Brāhmaṇa named Somaśarman, proficient in Sāmaveda, and the issue of this marriage was Hiraṇya-varman, indicating the use of the epithet Varman in a Brāhmaṇa family. The Brahma-kṣatra *vaṁśa* is referred to in an inscription of the eighth century A.D. (No. 49).

The reference to Bhavavarman's sister as '*pativratā*' and *dharmaratā* (devoted to husband and religion) like a second Arundhatī indicates that the high Indian ideal of womanhood was carried to these colonies. The great prominence given to sister's sons in several inscriptions (Nos. 27, 30) seems to indicate the prevalence of matriarchy, though nothing can be definitely asserted on this point.[23]

Unfortunately the inscriptions do not throw much light on the life of the common people. The Chinese chronicle, however, gives us a lot of interesting information about it. The following extracts from the History of the Sui dynasty describe the manners and customs of the people of Kambuja at the beginning of the seventh century:—

[Marriage]: 'They present the bride a robe. The families of bridegroom and bride stay for 8 days at home and keep lamps burning day and night. After marriage the husband takes a portion of his ancestral property and lives in a separate house with his wife'.

[Funeral ceremony]: 'The children of the deceased do not eat or shave for seven days and utter loud cries. The relations, with the priests and priestesses, carry the dead with prayers and music, burn the body with all kinds of aromatic woods, put the ashes in an urn of gold and silver and throw it in a big river. The poor use earthen jar painted in different colours. Sometimes they do not burn the body but leave it in the hills to be devoured by beasts'.

[Epidemics]: 'To prevent epidemics, sacrifices are offered beyond the western gates of the town by killing pigs, bulls and lambs

23. Later inscriptions of Kambuja refer more directly to the succession through females, a custom still prevalent in Laos (*Corpus*, pp. 124-126, 179-80).

of white colour. They believe that otherwise grains will not ripen, domestic animals will die and large number of people would fall victim to epidemic'.

[General nature and habits]: 'The men are short and have a dark complexion. But there are white women. The people dress their hair and wear ear-rings. They consider the right hand as pure and the left impure. Every morning they make ablutions, cleanse teeth by small pieces of branches of trees, read books, say prayers, again make ablution, take food, cleanse teeth after meal, and again say prayers. Their food includes a large quantity of butter, cream, sugar and millet (in the form of cake or bread). Before meal they take some morsels of roasted meat with bread, which they eat with a little salt'.

The following statement about Kambuja, in the History of the T'ang dynasty, probably refers to the seventh century: —

'The houses are all turned towards the east. They welcome the guests with areca, camphor and perfumes, for they do not drink publicly but only with their own wives at home avoiding the presence of parents'.

In spite of the fragmentary nature of the information we have culled above from the Chinese chronicles and epigraphic evidence, the dominance of Indian influence in the development of culture and civilisation in Kambuja is clearly manifest. This is only what could be expected in a country colonised by the Indians. It may be safely presumed that they maintained regular contact with their motherland. The king Īśānavarman, for example, is specifically referred to in an Inscription (No. 16) to have relations with India. But the most striking evidence of a continuous contact with India and of her serving as the perennial spring which fed the fountain of Indian culture in Kambuja is furnished by the development of Indian art in that far-off colony, to which a brief reference has already been made in the last lecture.

LECTURE IV.

THE CONSOLIDATION OF THE KAMBUJA KINGDOM

SECTION 1. THE DARK PERIOD

The seventh century A.D. witnessed the rise of Kambuja as a great political power and a flourishing centre of Hindu culture and civilisation. But its history during the eighth century A.D. is shrouded in darkness and obscurity. A few isolated epigraphic data and a brief account preserved in the Chinese chronicles enable us to form a very vague idea of its general condition, but it is impossible to give any connected outline of its political history during the century following the reign of Jayavarman I, the last known king who ruled over the kingdom founded by Bhavavarman I. The only certain information that we may derive is that the mighty and extensive kingdom over which the dynasty of Bhavavarman ruled had been divided into a number of states, and we possess the names of a few of them and some of their rulers. But the location of these states and the names and order of succession of their rulers, far less their activities, cannot be definitely ascertained. The eighth century A.D. may thus be justly described as the dark period of the history of Kambuja, fortunately the only dark period in its almost unchequered history of thousand years. All that we can do, so far as this period is concerned, is to bring together such evidences as we possess and try to correlate them as far as available materials permit.

According to the Chinese annals of the Tang Dynasty, shortly after 705–706 A.D., i.e. at the beginning of the eighth century A.D., Chen-la or Kambuja was divided into two states, viz., Kambuja of the land and Kambuja of the water. The former, called also Wen-tan or Po-leu, comprised the northern part of Cambodia, full of hills and valleys, and the latter covered the southern part which bordered on the sea and abounded in lakes and streams.[1] Ma-Tuan-Lin confirms this account and adds that Chen-la or Kambuja of the water had an extent of 800 *li* and that its king inhabited the town of Po-lo-ti-pa.[2] Until recently the

1. *BEFEO*. XXXVI, p. 1.
2. *Ibid*, p. 5.

Chinese account was taken to mean that the Kambuja proper was divided into two kingdoms, and attempts were made by various scholars to define the boundaries of, or at least to locate, these two kingdoms which the Chinese so characteristically referred to as Kambuja of land and Kambuja of water. The fact, however, appears to be that by Chen-la or Kambuja of the land the Chinese referred to a kingdom to the north of Kambuja proper, including a great part of Laos and touching the Chinese province of Tonkin and the Thai kingdom of Yunnan. This kingdom maintained diplomatic relations with China and sent an embassy to the Imperial court in 717 A.D. But five years later we find this kingdom sending an army to help Mei Hiuan-Cheng, the frontier chief of Nghe-an in Annam who had revolted against the Chinese emperor and was joined by several other chiefs of hilly regions. The Kambuja army joined the rebel chief of Annam and defeated the Chinese forces.[2a] This incident shows that the northern Kambuja kingdom was a fairly powerful one.

The friendly relations of the kingdom with China were, however, soon restored, and an embassy was sent in 750 A.D. In 753 A.D. the son of the king visited the Chinese Court with a retinue of 26 persons and accompanied the Chinese military expedition against Nan-chao. In 771 the king Po-mi paid a visit to the Chinese Emperor. The last embassy to China was sent in 799 A.D. In spite of these frequent references, the Chinese accounts do not enable us to precisely determine the location of the kingdom. It appears, however, from the itinerary of Kia Tan, that in the eighth century the nominal suzerainty of China was extended as far as Laos, and Wen-tan, or Kambuja of the land, touched the Chinese province of Tonkin. This indicates that Wen-tan extended along the middle course of the Mekong.[3]

As regards Chen-la of water or the Kambuja proper we know the names of a few kingdoms and their rulers from the inscriptions of king Yaśovarman who flourished towards the close of the ninth century A.D. These records begin with a genealogical account of the king the first part of which may be summed up as follows:[4]

"There was a descendant of the lord of Aninditapura, Śrī Puṣkarākṣa by name, who obtained the kingdom of Śambhupura.

2a. *BEFEO.* XVIII, No. 3, pp. 29-30.

3. *BEFEO,* IV. pp. 211-12.

4. *Corpus,* p. 364.

Rājendravarman, who was born in the family of this king and whose mother was descended from the suzerains (*adhirāja*) of Vyādhapura, also ruled in Śambhupura".

The first part of this genealogy is further elucidated by that of Rājendravarman given in Pre-Rup Ins. (No. 93) and Mebon Ins. (No. 89A). According to these, Puṣkarākṣa was the son of king Nṛpatīndravarman who was descended from Sarasvatī, the sister's daughter of Bālāditya, king of Aninditapura and a descendant of Kauṇḍinya and Somā. These relationships may be shown by the following genealogical table:[5]

Kauṇḍinya = Somā

Bālāditya   D
|
Sarasvatī = Viśvarūpa
:
Nṛpatīndravarman
|
Puṣkarākṣa

Of the three kingdoms mentioned in this extract the location of Śambhupura admits of no doubt. It is represented by modern Sambor on the Mekong.[6]

As regards Vyādhapura, Aymonier's identification of it with Ankor Borei in the province of Prei Krebas held the ground till Coedès demonstrated that it was more probably situated at the foot of the hill called Ba Phnom and possibly this kingdom represented that of ancient Fu-nan.[7]

The site of Aninditapura is not definitely known, but according to Coedès it must be looked for in the region east of Angkor on the north side of the Great Lake (Tonle Sap).[8]

The somewhat curious and pompous genealogy of Yaśovarman, recorded at length in identical words in a large number of his inscriptions (Nos. 60-63), is an elaborate attempt to connect that ruler, however remotely, with the three ruling families of Kambuja. Whatever historical truth there may be in this genea-

5. *Inscriptions*, pp. 74-75.
6. *Aymonier*, I. p. 309.
7. *BEFEO*. XXVIII. pp. 127-131.
8. *Ibid*, p. 133.

logical pedigree, these official documents leave no doubt that towards the close of the ninth century A.D., when they were drawn up, the three royal families of old times occupied a position of eminence in the memory of the people.

The first question, therefore, that arises in this connection is whether there is any independent evidence that Śambhupura, Aninditapura and Vyādhapura flourished as independent kingdoms in the eighth century A. D.

Following the interpretation of Yaśovarman's records by Bergaigne it is generally held that Rājendravarman, the great-grandfather of Yāśovarman, married the heiress of the kingdom of Vyādhapura and thus added that kingdom to his own. But this interpretation is not justified by the language of the records which merely says that Rājendravarman's wife was descended from the suzerains of Vyādhapura.[9] If we uphold the identification of Vyādhapura with the old kingdom of Fu-nan, the reference to it in Yaśovarman's genealogy might mean no more than a claim to have been descended from the old royal family of Fu-nan which ruled over Cambodia till the middle of the sixth century A.D. Further, we should remember that the term *adhirāja* (suzerain), applied to the rulers of Vyādhapura, would be more appropriate to the king of old Fu-nan, than to the local ruler of a petty state. It is, therefore, difficult to admit the existence of Vyādhapura as a kingdom in the eighth century A.D. on the basis of evidence so far available to us.[10]

We are perhaps more fortunate in the cases of the other two kingdoms. An inscription (No. 48) discovered at Prah That Kvan Pir, and dated in 638 Śaka (=716 A.D.), states that one Puṣkara had a god Puṣkareśa consecrated by the ascetics and Brahmans. This Puṣkara has been identified with Puṣkarākṣa,[11] mentioned in the genealogical accounts of Yaśovarman and Rājendravarman, who was a descendant of Bālāditya, king of Aninditapura, and obtained (probably by marriage) the kingdom of Śambhupura. The existence of these two kingdoms in the eighth century A.D., and even earlier, may thus be provisionally admitted. If the genealogical account of Yaśovarman is to be fully believed, we must hold that these kingdoms were united,

9. *Ibid*, p. 126 f.n. (2).
10. *Ibid*, p. 130.
11. *BEFEO*. IV, p. 214.

temporarily or permanently we cannot say, in the first half of the eighth century A.D.

Three inscriptions[12] found in Cochin-China throw further light on this question. One of them, found at Thap Musi, refers to the installation of (an image or temple of) god Śrī-Puṣkarākṣa by king Śambhuvarman. The temple of Puṣkarākṣa is also referred to in the second inscription found in the same place which records the installation of an image of Puspavaṭasvāmī in the sanctuary of Mūlasthāna. The third inscription found at the foot of the hill Nui Ba-the, in the district of Lon-Xuyen, refers to the construction of a brick temple on the top of the hill for the Vardhamāna-Liṅga (of Śiva) for increasing the religious merit of king Śrī Nṛpāditya.

Now, there can be no question that both Śambhuvarman and Nṛpāditya, whose records have been found in Cochin-China, ruled in what the Chinese call Kambuja of the water. The name-ending *āditya* of the second king, in contrast to the *varman*, almost universally found in Kambuja may indicate his association with Bālāditya king of Aninditapura, referred to above. If we presume such a connection, the kingdom of Aninditapura may be regarded as corresponding to the Kambuja of the water. Po-lo-ti-po, the capital of the latter, according to the Chinese Annals, may then be restored as Bālādityapura after the name of Bālāditya. But whatever one might think of this, it is less difficult to connect Śambhuvarman with Śambhupura, on the analogy of other towns named after the king, such as Bhavapura, Śreṣṭhapura, Īśānapura, etc.

The fact that inscriptions of both Śambhuvarman and Nṛpāditya are found in the same region naturally connect these two kings, and if we accept the hypothesis that the latter was connected with Bālāditya, we may find here a confirmation of the statement in the records of Yaśovarman, referred to above, according to which Puṣkarākṣa united the two kingdoms of Aninditapura and Śambhupura. Further, it is interesting to note that two of the three inscriptions in Cochin-China referred to above mention the God Puṣkarākṣa, who may after all owe this designation to the king of that name, who would thus be closely related to the other two kings, as suggested in the records of Yaśovarman.

Thus although no definite conclusion is possible, we may accept, as a provisional hypothesis, that shortly after the death of

12. For the text of these inscriptions and the inferences drawn from them cf. *BEFEO*. XXXVI, pp. 3 ff.

Jayavarman I, Kambuja was split up into two kingdoms with Śambhupura and Aninditapura respectively as their capitals. The fact that the rulers of Aninditapura regarded themselves as descended from Kauṇḍinya and Somā, shows that the old traditions of Fu-nan, carried over by Bhavavarman and his successors, were still continued, and for all we know there might have been some sort of relationship between the royal family of Aninditapura and that of Bhavavarman.

Unfortunately we possess no detailed account of any of the two kingdoms of Śambhupura and Aninditapura. In addition to the names of kings, mentioned above, who ruled over these kingdoms, in the eighth century A.D., the records of Yaśovarman and his father Indravarman furnish names of other kings as will be noted in connection with their history.[13] But when and where they ruled, it is difficult to say. The names of a few other kings are supplied by a Khmer inscription dated 725 S. (803 A.D.) (No. 50). It refers to a religious endowment by the queen Jyeṣṭhāryā, and names, as her ancestors, the king Jayendra, the queen Nṛpendradevī and the king Śrī Indraloka. As the inscription is engraved on a temple at Sambor, these rulers may be regarded as kings of Śambhupura.

Attempts have been made to identify the two kingdoms of Kambuja, referred to in the Chinese annals, with those mentioned in epigraphic records. Until recently it was generally held that the kingdom of Śambhupura corresponded to the Kambuja of land, and that of Vyādhapura, to the Kambuja of water of the Chinese chronicles. Coedès, however, dissented from this view and at first identified the last with Aninditapura. He now holds that the Kambuja of water more probably corresponded to the kingdom of Aninditapura, united with that of Śambhupura, while Kambuja of land denoted the territory north of Dangrek mountains.[14]

Whatever we might think of these theories, there is no doubt about the fact that during the eighth century A.D. Kambuja had lost the unity and solidarity which were imparted to it by the conquests of Bhavavarman and his successors, and was split up into two or possibly more states, none of which was evidently of any considerable power or importance. Such a state of things could, of course, have been brought about by natural causes. But indications are not wanting that the fate of Kambuja was at least partly determined by external events.

13. See pp. 91-92.

14. *BEFEO.* XXXVI, 1 ff. where the older views, even other than those

The most outstanding fact in the political history of Indo-China and Indonesia in the eighth century A.D. is the rise of the Śailendras as a great power.[15] Their empire included Sumatra, Java, Malay Peninsula and a large number of islands in the Indian archipelago There is no doubt that the northern part of Malay Peninsula constituted a stronghold of their power and thus they were too dangerously near the western frontier of the Kambuja kingdom. Although positive evidence is lacking, there are reasonable grounds to suppose that the Śailendras extended their supremacy over Kambuja. In any case there is no doubt that Kambuja was a vassal state of Java towards the close of the eighth century A.D. when that island itself was at least partially conquered by the Śailendras.

As a matter of fact we can trace Javanese influence over Kambuja from the beginning of the eighth century A.D. King Sañjaya of Java is mentioned in his inscription, dated 732 A.D., as a conqueror of the countries of neighbouring kings. This somewhat vague statement is corroborated by a detailed list of conquests of the king in a literary work. After mentioning conquests in Java and Bali islands, this text refers to his over-seas expedition in course of which he proceeded to the Malaya country and fought with Kemir and other powers.[16] There is no doubt that Kemir stands here for the Khmers or the people of Kambuja. Ordinarily the value of such references may be discounted to a certain extent in view of the well-known tendency of the court-poets to exaggerate the achievements of their royal patrons. But in this particular instance the record of Kambuja itself supports the theory of a Javanese conquest of Kambuja. For, an inscription in Kambuja (No. 151) which we shall have occasion to discuss in details later, refers to a Kambuja king, who ruled towards the beginning of the ninth century A.D., as having come from Java and performed a religious ceremony in order that Kambuja might not again be dependent on Java.

The dependence of Kambuja on Java during the latter half of the eighth century A.D. is also indirectly supported by the reference in the inscriptions of Champā to Javanese naval raids on the coast of Annam as far as Tonkin in the north. An inscription dated 784 A.D. says that in 774 A.D. ferocious people of other

15. *Suvarṇadvīpa*, I, Bk. II. Ch. I.
16. *Ibid*, p. 230.

cities came in ships and burnt a temple of Śiva at Kauṭhāra (S. Annam) and carried the Mukhaliṅga of the god. Another inscription dated 799 A.D. states that a temple was burnt by the army of Java coming by means of ships and became empty in the Śaka year 709 (=787 A.D.). The Chinese annals also refer to an invasion of the northern part of Annam by the people of Daba, which Maspero identifies with Java, in 767 A.D. These successive naval raids by Java may be taken to indicate some control over the Kambuja kingdom. It is interesting to note in this connection a story recorded by Merchant Sulayman about the Mahārāja, king of Zābag, an expression by which the Arab writers meant the Śailendra Emperor. "It is said that once the Khmer king remarked to his minister that he would like to see the head of the king of Zābag before him in a dish. The Mahārāja, having heard of this, secretly equipped one thousand vessels full of soldiers and invaded Khmer. The king of Khmer knew nothing of the impending danger until the hostile fleet had entered the river which led to his capital and landed its troops. The Mahārāja thus took the king of Khmer unawares, seized upon his palace and cut off his head."[17] The story undoubtedly belongs to the domain of folk-lore but may have been based on a real struggle between Zābag and the Khmer kingdom of Kambuja. It is needless for our present purpose to discuss whether Sañjaya, the king of Java, belonged to the Śailendra dynasty or not, and whether the naval raids on Champā are to be credited to the Śailendras or to some other kings of Java. It seems to be clear, however, that Java, under either the Śailendras or some other royal dynasty, exercised political supremacy over Kambuja at least for a time during the eighth century A.D. This sufficiently explains the dismemberment of the political fabric that Bhavavarman and his successors had reared in Java. The political association between Java and Kambuja perhaps also accounts for some of the striking features which we note in the subsequent history of Kambuja, specially the influence of Tantric religion and the great building activities,—two features which characterised Javanese culture at that time. The removal of the capital of Kambuja from the bank of the Mekong river to inland cities might also, not improbably, have been due to the fear of Javanese naval power. But these are all mere speculations for the present, as the history of Kambuja, during this period, is shrouded in darkness and no definite conclusion can be arrived at on these and other analogous points.

17. *Ibid*, pp. 156-159.

SECTION 2. JAYAVARMAN II & III

The obscurity which envelops the history of Kambuja for more than a century after the death of Jayavarman I is removed with the accession of Jayavarman II at the beginning of the ninth century A.D. or shortly before it. The history of Kambuja once more emerges into light, and we can trace her rulers in an unbroken line of succession down to modern times. Kambuja not only becomes free and united but grows in power and prestige till it becomes the nucleus of a mighty empire and the centre of a glorious civilisation whose monuments still excite the wonder of the world. This undoubtedly accounts for the great honour and esteem in which the name of Jayavarman II was held by posterity even centuries later, when everything else about ancient Kambuja had faded out of memory.

This enthusiasm and reverence for Jayavarman II are also shared by modern historians of Kambuja who represent Jayavarman II in brilliant limelight and depict him as a great builder and a powerful conqueror. Some of the most magnificent monuments of Kambuja have been attributed to him and he has been credited with brilliant and successful military campaigns far and wide. But this complacent belief has been somewhat shaken in recent years by fresh facts brought to light, and it is a task of no mean difficulty now to write a critical account of his life and times in a detached spirit. But this task has to be faced, and the question must be treated at some length, in order to put the history of Kambuja on a firm foundation.

There is not a single record of Jayavarman II.[1] The earliest reference to him occurs in the inscriptions of Yaśovarman who ascended the throne nearly half a century after the death of Jayavarman II. Besides some vague and general expressions about his great power and suzerainty over many kings, these inscriptions (cf. No. 60) contain two facts of historical importance. In the first place the genealogical account contained in them shows that Jayavarman's grandmother (mother's mother) was a niece (sister's daughter) of king Puskarākṣa who, as mentioned above, was the king of Śambhupura and Aninditapura, and Jayavarman's queen was the niece (sister's daughter) of king Rudravarman. Secondly,

1. The Ins. of Labok Srot (No. 49), dated 703 S', has been referred to him by Coedès, but this is very doubtful. The point has been discussed later.

we are told that Jayavarman II fixed his residence on the Mahendra mountain. An inscription (No. 93) of Rājendravarman, who flourished half a century after Yaśovarman, adds only the name of the father of Puṣkarākṣa, viz. king Śrī Nṛpatīndravarman. Half a century later still, an inscription of Sūryavarman (No. 148) mentions 724 Śaka (=802 A.D.) as the date of the accession of Jayavarman II and gives the name of his queen as Pavitrā.[2] It is not till we come to the reign of Udayādityavarman, about the middle of the eleventh century A.D., that we get the only detailed account, that we so far possess, about the life and reign of Jayavarman II, from the Sdok Kak Thom Ins. (No. 151). In view of the importance of this inscription, not only from the point of view of the history of Jayavarman II, but also as throwing very interesting light on the influence of the royal priests in affairs of state, it is necessary to give a short account of its contents.

It is a very long record of 340 lines which contain 130 verses in Sanskrit and 146 lines of prose text in the native Khmer language. Its author was a Brāhmaṇa, Sadāśiva by name, who was the High Priest of the Royal family and whose ancestors filled the same post from the time of Jayavarman II (802 A.D.) up to the year 1052 A.D. when the record was drawn up. It gives the names of the kings whom they served, and we thus find here not only the royal names from Jayavarman II to Udayādityavarman II in an unbroken line of succession, but also the names of all the High Priests of the Tutelary Deity of Kambuja with a catalogue of the pious works and religious foundations of each of them, and a list of the royal favours in the shape of honours, dignities, grant of lands etc., which each received from his royal patron. Such an interesting history of a sacerdotal family, extending over a period of 250 years, is perhaps without a parallel in the history of India and her colonies abroad. This history is first recorded in Sanskrit and then repeated in Khmer with some variations and additional details.

The most interesting part of this record, for our present purpose, is the account it gives of the establishment of the cult of Devarāja by Jayavarman II and of the first appointment of a High Priest of this cult with a royal decree making the office hereditary in his family. As the whole career of Jayavarman II is narrated

2. Barth infers from an Inscription of Indravarman (No. 56) that Dharanīndradevī was the name of a queen of Jayavarman II (*Corpus*, pp. 301-3). His arguments are not, however, convincing.

in this connection we may quote the relevant passage in Khmer which runs as follows:—

"The family was dwelling in the village of Bhadrayogin in the district of Indrapura. Jayavarman II came from Java to reign in the city of Indrapura. The venerable Guru Śivakaivalya became his royal priest. Then His Majesty left Indrapura, and Śivakaivalya accompanied him....Having arrived at Viṣaya Pūrvadiśa he gave lands to Śivakaivalya and his family who followed him there. He also founded a village called Kuṭi and assigned it to them.... Then His Majesty reigned in the city of Hariharālaya. Śivakaivalya also settled there with his family. ....Then the king founded the city of Amarendrapura, and Śivakaivalya also settled there for serving His Majesty. Then the king went to reign at Mahendraparvata. Śivakaivalya also resided there. There His Majesty invited a Brāhmaṇa named Hiraṇyadāma, versed in magic, in order to perform some Tantric rites so that Kambujadeśa might no longer be dependent on Java and have a paramount ruler (*cakravartī*) of its own. This Brāhmaṇa, who came from Janapada (probably in India), performed some Tantric rites (which are described in detail) and the worship of Devarāja. He also initiated Śivakaivalya into these rituals and taught him the sacred books dealing with them. Śivakaivalya, in his turn, taught them to all his relations, and the king took a vow to employ only the family of Śivakaivalya and none else to celebrate the worship of Devarāja. Then His Majesty returned to Hariharālaya and reigned there till his death. Śivakaivalya also died during his reign. His Majesty had brought Devarāja to Hariharālaya, and his successors took the god to various capitals which they founded in course of time, as he was regarded as the protector of the realm."[3]

3. It is very difficult to form a clear and prceise idea of the cult of Devarāja. It seems to be the designation of the *liṅga* (of Śiva) which represented the essence of the royal authority conceived as divine and, being regarded as the tutelary deity, was placed in a temple on the top of a mountain, or on the summit of a pyramidal construction, representing Kailāsa, the abode of the gods (*Melanges, S. Levi*, pp. 200-202). On the other hand indications are not wanting that Devarāja denoted not merely, or not so much, a particular *liṅga*, as a ritual or ceremony, Tantrik in character. This, at any rate, seems to follow from the Ins. No. 151. For a full discussion on this point cf. *BEFEO* XXXIV. pp. 611-16. Bosch holds that a cult similar to Devarāja existed in Java (*BEFEO.* XXV. p. 391; *TBG.* LXIV, p. 227). If so, it is probable that Jayavarman II derived his knowledge and inspiration about it from that country where he resided for some time before occupying the throne of Kambuja.

Leaving aside for the present the question how far we may rely on statements recorded two hundred and fifty years after the events they relate, we shall now proceed to reconstruct the history of Jayavarman on the basis of the data supplied by the above extract.

It is obvious at the very outset that Jayavarman II did not inherit the kingdom in a normal way. He resided for some time in Java, for reasons or under circumstances not known to us, and then returned to his native land which was under the domination of a foreign power ruling in Java. He freed the land from the foreign yoke and even went to the length of performing religious rites to ensure the continuity of its newly gained independence. It is probable that he was sent by the suzerain power to rule Kambuja as a vassal chief, and found opportunity to proclaim his independence. But we have no definite information on this point, and other explanations are possible. What seems to be certain is that by some means or other he established an independent kingdom in Kambuja.[4]

That Jayavarman II did not secure the throne by right of birth seems to follow also from the genealogical accounts of Yaśovarman and Rājendravarman to which reference has already been made above. It is true that according to the genealogy both Jayavarman and his queen were related to the royal families of Kambuja. For Puṣkarākṣa, the first ancestor of Yaśovarman mentioned in these accounts, and who ruled over both Śambhupura and Aninditapura, is said to have been the maternal uncle of the maternal uncle of the mother of king Jayavarman II. The genealogical accounts of Yaśovarman further tell us that the mother of the queen of Jayavarman II was the maternal aunt of king Pṛthivīndravarman who was the father of Indravarman and grandfather of Yaśovarman. But the very fact that even the genealogy drawn up in the royal court could show no better claim to throne either for Jayavarman II or his queen amounts almost to a positive evidence that he or his queen had no such claim worth mentioning. For nobody can pretend that these relationships, even if accepted as true, would make Jayavarman II the natural or legitimate heir to the throne. It is probable that they were recorded, perhaps even devised, in

4. Maspero (pp. 28-29) has put forward some suggesitons, but they must be regarded as more hypotheses.

later times to give an appearance of legitimacy to the claim of Jayavarman upon the throne of Kambuja which he had actually seized by some means or other. That Jayavarman II did not ascend the throne by right of heredity may also be concluded from verse 8 of the Phnom Sandak Ins. (No. 69) recorded in 817 Ś (=895 A.D.). The royal race to which he belonged is therein described as the great lotus stalk which did not rise from the soil, and he is said to have risen like a fresh lotus for the prosperity of his subjects. Barth has pointed out that this evidently alluded to a change of dynasty, and this view appears quite reasonable.

On the other hand a casual reference in Ins. No. 58 (v. 30) to Jayendrādhipativarman as maternal uncle of Jayavarman II might indicate some legitimate claim to the throne. We do not know the exact status of Jayendrādhipati, nor have we any idea whether he had any male issue, but considering the importance of daughters in matters of succession in Kambuja, Jayavarman II might have some real claim to the throne through his mother. An inscription (No. 50) dated 803 A.D. records the donations of queen Jyeṣṭhāryā and mentions Jayendra, queen Nṛpendradevī and king Śrīndraloka. Jayendra may be identified with Jayendrādhipativarman, and as the date falls early in the reign of Jayavarman II, it may be held that the former did not reign long before. In other words, Jayavarman II may be presumed to have had legitimate claim to the kingdom of Śambhupura, the region where this inscription was found, as the successor of Jayendrādhipativarman.

But, howsoever he might have come to the throne, the most important and interesting point is his frequent change of capitals. The location of the towns named is not free from difficulty, and we may briefly refer to the current views on the subject.[5]

1. Indrapura.—From the data supplied by an inscription found at Phum Mien Coedès locates Indrapura in the district of Khbong Khmum in the Kompong Cham Division. He suggests that the actual site of the town is now represented by Bantay Prei Nokor whose name indicates it to be an ancient royal capital, and the monuments of which, although belonging to the primitive period of Khmer art, shows the influence of classical art in some details.

5. Cf. discussion by Coedès (*BEFEO*. XXVIII. pp. 113 ff.) and P. Stern (ibid. XXXVIII. pp. 175 ff.)

On the other hand P. Stern locates Indrapura at Baray near Angkor.

2. Kuṭi, in the Viṣaya (district) Pūrvadiśa. This was probably situated to the east of Angkor Thom and Coedès holds, in common with Aymonier, that the name is still preserved in Bantay Kdei, though its famous temple is later in date.[6]

3. Hariharālaya.—Aymonier's identification of this city with Prah Khan, immediately to the north of Angkor Thom, had been generally accepted. Coedès pointed out that the inscriptions attribute a number of monuments to Indravarman who lived in Hariharālaya throughout his reign, and that these monuments are all to be found in a group, known as Roluos, 13 miles to the south-east of Angkor. He therefore provisionally located Hariharālaya in this region[7] and traced even a feeble echo of the last part of this name in modern Lolei. This theory has now been fully confirmed by the inscription of Kok Svay Prahm (No. 102).

4. Amarendrapura.—Here again Aymonier's identification of this capital with Bantay Chmar (100 miles to the north-west of Angkor Thom), and the attribution of the famous monument of that place to Jayavarman II, generally accepted by previous writers, have been challenged by M. Stern and others. Coedès holds the view that although the monument is later than the time of Jayavarman II, the site of Amarendrapura must be looked for in the neighbourhood, i.e., in the northern part of the province of Battambang.

5. Mahendraparvata.—Aymoneir identified it with the Phnom Kulen (to the north-west of Angkor Thom), but the absence of any monument on the top of this hill led him to place the city of Jayavarman at the foot of the hill amidst the ruins of Beng Mala. For the same reason Finot proposed its identification with Prah Khan. But the hill top contains some brick towers (Prasat Damrei Krap and a few other small brick buildings) intermediate in style between the primitive Khmer art and that of Indravarman. And this is all that we could expect in the reign of Jayavarman II according to the modern view of the evolution of Khmer art. The

6. For an account of the locality and its three ancient temples, called Kuṭiśvara, cf. *BEFEO*. XXXVII. pp. 333 cf.

7. This is confirmed by the recent archaeological researches (*BEFEO*. XXXVI. p. 630).

location of Jayavarman's city on the top of the Phnom Kulen may, therefore, be accepted.[8]

If the above identifications are accepted it would follow that immediately after his return from Java Jayavarman fixed his capital at Indrapura, not far from the ancient royal seat of Śambhupura. It is noteworthy that an inscription[9] found near this city records the construction of gates of the temple of the Lord of Śambhupura by four relations of Jayavarman II. It is, therefore, reasonable to conclude that Jayavarman II himself was a native of that region and naturally set up his first capital in its neighbourhood. But then we find a gradual change of royal seat towards the west, first towards Angkor, then further west towards Battambang, and lastly again back to Angkor. Were these changes merely due to royal caprices, or inspired by a desire to find a suitable site for the capital of the newly founded kingdom? It is difficult to accept any of these views, though they have found favour with scholars. For all we know it may be a sign of weakness, or indication of troubles which forced the king to take refuge in different parts of the country. Considering the past history of Kambuja, and the almost certain fact that Jayavarman II had no legitimate claim to this kingdom, nothing is more natural than to suppose that his accession to power was not peacefully secured, and he had to pass many years in constant troubles which forced him almost to a nomadic court-life as Coedés very aptly describes it. In any case this is not a less reasonable hypothesis than any of the other two noted above. In that case our view about the life and reign of Jayavarman II would undergo almost a radical change. Instead of regarding him as a grand monarch who united the whole of Kambuja into a powerful kingdom, set up successive capitals in different parts of the kingdom, and endowed them with palaces and temples whose ruins lie scattered in the sites of those cities, we have to look upon him as an adventurer who managed to set up as an independent king but had to strive hard almost the whole of his life to secure the position he had gained against other possible rivals. What has been visualised as a foundation of beautiful capitals, one after another, may be no more than seeking refuge in distant corners of his kingdom against powerful foes.

8. This, too, has been confirmed by recent archaeological researches (*BEFEO*. XXXVI. p. 630).

9. Aymonier I. 307.

A somewhat more favourable view is to suppose that the frequent change of capitals was the result of the chaotic political condition of Kambuja at the time of Jayavarman's return from Java. Perhaps it took him many years to bring the whole kingdom under his control. Beginning with his native kingdom of Śambhupra in the east, he gradually proceeded westwards, and the different capitals may merely indicate the different stages of political consolidation. Ultimately when the whole country was subdued, he fixed his final capital at Hariharālaya in the central part of the kingdom.

A possible source of trouble for Kambuja at this period has generally been overlooked by scholars. The Po Nagar Inscription of Harivarman,[10] king of Champā, refers to one of his generals as having ravaged Kambuja and forcibly advanced up to the very heart of the kingdom. This inscription being dated in year 739 Śaka, the incident must have taken place at the beginning of the ninth century A.D., i.e. early in the reign of Jayavarman II. It is not impossible, therefore, that the Cham incursions forced Jayavarman to leave Indrapura and even the Angkor region, and betake himself to the western part of the kingdom. It was only when that menace was over that he could again come back to the Angkor region and spend his last years in his capital Hariharālaya. The final choice of this capital, in place of the old Indrapura, was perhaps also influenced by the same consideration, viz., to remove the seat of the capital from the dangerous neighbourhood of the border of Champā. All these are possible interpretations of the few facts that the record of the priestly family has preserved to posterity and, according as we accept one or the other, we shall have to view the life and reign of Jayavarman II in altogether different lights. Thus if we hold that all the capital cities were in his possession at one and the same time, we must hold that he reigned over the whole of Kambuja, and brought about the unity of the country after the lapse of more than a century. But this has to be considerably modified if any of the other interpretations be accepted.

Similar uncertainty prevails about the date of Jayavarman's accession. This is all the more to be regretted as until recently it was definitely fixed at 724 Śaka (=802 A.D.) and the scholars re-

10. *Champa*, Bk. III, p. 61; *Corpus*, p. 263.

garded it as a sheet-anchor in Kambuja chronology. This date is furnished by several inscriptions of Yaśovarman and Sūryavarman. But the great French scholar Coedés has drawn attention to an inscription in the temple of Labok Srot (No. 49) which was issued in the reign of king Jayavarman and is dated in the year 703 Śaka (=781 A.D.). Coedés, while first editing the inscription, shared the general view that Jayavarman II came to the throne in 724 Śaka, and hence regarded king Jayavarman of this inscription as a different king. But he now proposes to take this inscription as belonging to the reign of Jayavarman II and thus pushes back the date of his accession by more than twenty years.[11] Coedés reconciles this view with the data of the later inscriptions by interpreting the date 724 Śaka furnished by them as that of the establishment of the capital of Jayavarman II on Mahendraparvata, an event which according to the Sdok Kok Thom inscription (No. 151) must have taken place many years after his accession to the throne.

In view of the great scholarship of M. Coedés and his unrivalled knowledge of Kambuja history any hypothesis propounded by him commands our respect and attention. But it is difficult to subscribe to his present view about the date of Jayavarman II. For there seems to be hardly any justification for taking 724 Śaka as the date of the capital on Mahendraparvata. It is true that the qualifying phrase '*Mahendr-ādri-sthiti*' is often applied to Jayavarman II along with the date, but it should more properly be regarded as qualifying the king, and it is a too far-fetched construction to take it along with the date. Moreover, in certain inscriptions, the passage containing the date omits all reference to Mahendraparvata. Thus the Prāsāt Kèv. Ins. (No. 148) has "*Āsīd Kambuja-rājendro veda-dvi-nāga-rājya-bhāk,*" and this may be compared with another verse in the same Inscription "*Āsīd Śrī—Sūrya-Varmmeti veda-dvi-vila-rājya-bhāk.*" There can be no question that the latter gives the date 924 for the accession of Sūryavarman. The identical words in the other verse should not be interpreted differently and we should therefore hold that Jayavarman II came to the throne in 724 Ś (=802 A.D.).[12]

11. *BEFEO*. XXVIII. p. 119.

12. The Prasat Kok Po Ins. (No. 123, *BEFEO* XXXVII. p. 389) also refers to the date of the accession of Jayavarman II without any reference to Mahendraparvata. The question has been recently discussed by me in *JGIS.*, X. p. 52.

But if we are unable to accept M. Coedés' view about the date of Jayavarman's accession, his new theory about the date of his death certainly appears to be the most reasonable hypothesis.[13] The generally accepted view that Jayavarman II died in 791 Śaka (869 A.D.) is based on Aymonier's interpretation of the Kok Rosei Ins. This inscription contains a date for the accession of a king, but as the first part of both is missing, we only know that a certain king, whose name ended in Varman, ascended the throne in the Śaka year 91 of an unknown century. Aymonier doubtfully read the first part of the name as Jaya, and argued that as the dates of accession of all the kings bearing the name Jayavarman, except that of Jayavarman III, are known, and none of them falls in the year 91 of any century, we must hold that Jayavarman III ascended the throne in 791 Ś, and consequently his father Jayavarman II died in that year. This view was generally accepted, but Coedés has very successfully demonstrated that the inscription in question must be referred to the reign of Jayavarman IV, and we shall discuss later his views about reconciling the date, which must now be read as 891, with the known date of his accession. In support of his view that the 791 Śaka cannot be regarded as the date of accession of Jayavarman III, Coedés has offered a new interpretation of the Prasat cak Ins. of Jayavarman dated the year 791 (No. 52). This inscription was regarded by all, including Coedés, as a definite confirmation of Aymonier's view, and an expression containing the words '16 years' was taken to refer to the age of the king. Coedés now interprets the expression to mean that the inscription was really engraved in the 16th year of the reign, and not when the king was 16 years old. This view seems to be quite reasonable, for while the inscriptions often refer to the regnal year it is very seldom, if ever, that they refer to the age of the king. Now, according to the new interpretation, 791 Śaka was the sixteenth regnal year of Jayavarman III, who must have, therefore, ascended the throne in 854 A.D. This view has since been confirmed by the discovery of Ins. No. 51 which gives the data 782 Ś for Jayavarman III. We may thus hold that Jayavarman II ruled from 802 to 854 A.D.

The names of Jayavarman's queens are known from several later Inscriptions. His chief queen (*agra-mahiṣī*), Pavitrā by

13. *BEFEO* XXVIII, pp. 113 ff.

name, is referred to in the Prea Kev Ins.[14] Another queen, Kambujalakṣmī, called also Prāṇa, is referred to in Phnom Prah Vihear Ins., which also refers to her relations as occupying high offices.[15] The Baku Ins. probably furnished the name of another queen Dharaṇīndradevī.[16] As we have seen above, one of the queens of Jayavarman II was related to a royal family, and she is expressly called the mother of Jayavarman III (orginally known as Jayavardhana).[17] Most probably she was the chief queen Pavitrā. Jayavarman had also a son by Kambujalakṣmī, Dharmavardhana by name.[18] An Ins. (No. 50), dated 725 Ś, refers to the donation of queen Jyeṣṭhāryā to Śiva. As the date falls in the reign of Jayavarman II, she may be another queen of the same king.

Jayavarman II revived the old tradition of Kambuja as against that of Fu-nan. As already noted above, Bhavavarman and his successors do not allude to the origin of the royal race of Kambuja from Kambu and Sūryavaṁśa, but refer instead to Kauṇḍinya and Somā as their ancestors like the kings of Fu-nan. Jayavarman's name is, however, associated with Kambu and Sūryavaṁśa. It is during his reign that an inscription of Champā[19] refers to the country as Kambuja, whereas an earlier inscription of the same kingdom, dated 657 A.D.,[20] refers to it as Bhavapura and associates it was Kauṇḍinya and Somā. Jayavarman is referred to in the inscriptions of his successors as 'Kambujarājendra' and "guardian of the honour of the solar race of king Kambu," and, as has just been mentioned, one of his queens bore the name or epithet Kambujalakṣmī. After him Kambujendra and Kambujeśvara became the normal official titles of the Khmer kings. Yaśovarman was particular in using these titles, and for a time at least the new capital city founded by him at Angkor Thom was known as Kambupurī. Similarly the later kings of Kambuja regard themselves as belonging to Sūryavaṁśa and not to Somavaṁśa. Thus Jayavarman's reign marks the revival of the old legendary origin of Kambuja and the end of the tradition of Fu-nan.

14. *Corpus*, p. 106.
15. *Ibid*, p. 539.
16. *Ibid*, p. 302.
17. *Ibid*, p. 365.
18. *Ibid*, p. 541.
19. *Champa*, Bk. III, p. 62.
20. *Ibid*, p. 23.

Like most other aspects of the career of Jayavarman II there is a great deal of controversy about his religion and artistic achievements. The views held on both these subjects have to be considerably modified in the light of recent researches.

It was believed that with Jayavarman began the golden age of Kambuja architecture. This belief was based mainly on the old identifications of the capitals of Jayavarman. For example, all the splendid monuments of Prah Khan were attributed to him as that was supposed to represent the site of Hariharālaya. Similarly the magnificent ruins of Beng Mala were regarded as those of his splendid monuments at Mahendraparvata. He was also regarded as having built the famous monuments at Bantay Chmar.[20a] These views must be given up now, and even if the identification of the old capitals still held good, we might well doubt whether all the fine buildings were constructed by Jayavarman II. But this does not mean that he did not build any noble monuments. The probability rather is that he did, though we do not know much of it. Popular tradition ascribes to him most of the grand monuments in ancient Kambuja. These are believed to have been erected by him with the help of an architect who was the son of a nymph and learned architecture from the gods in heaven. No other Kambuja king has left such a deep impress upon posterity as a great builder, and there must have been some basis on which the popular legend has grown up. It is a pity that our knowledge of his artistic activities is so meagre and uncertain. But we may well believe that he made a distinct contribution to the development of Kambuja architecture which reached such a high pitch of grandeur and excellence under his successors.

The view that Jayavarman II was a Buddhist similarly rests upon very weak foundations. This conclusion is based mainly on two grounds viz., that Jayavarman came from Java, which was a centre of Buddhism, and he founded Amarendrapura, now represented by Bantay Chmar, whose sculptures are predominantly Buddhist.[21] None of these proves much, and the identification in the latter case is open to doubt as mentioned above.

20a. Finot even suggested that Jayavarman began the construction of the great capital which bore later on the name of Yaśodharapura (*IHQ*. I, p. 615).
21. *IHQ*, I, p. 618.

The only positive evidence regarding the religious beliefs of Jayavarman II is furnished by the Sdok Kak Thom Inscription. (No. 151). Sivakaivalya, the royal priest, and the priestly family founded by him, which supplied royal chaplain for two hundred and fifty years, were undoubtedly Śaiva and presumably the king followed the same religion. The cult which he established as state religion with the help of the Brāhmaṇa Hiraṇyadāma seems to be a form of Tantric Śaivism. This follows from the detailed description of the magic rites contained in the Sdok Kak Thom Ins. It is said that the Brāhmaṇa Hiraṇyadāma performed the ritual as laid down in Vināśikha and consecrated the Devarāja cult. He taught Śivakaivalya the four texts known as Vināśikha, Nayottara, Saṁmoha and Śiraścheda. He recited these texts from beginning to end, so that they may be put in writing for the use of Śivakaivalya, and he taught the latter how to conduct the ritual of Devarāja. Later, we are told that these four texts constituted the four faces of Tumburu.

Now Dr. P. C. Bagchi has shown[22] that one of the four texts, viz. Nayottara, is definitely known to belong to the Āgama proper, i.e., the oldest Śaivite canon (which conformed to the Vedas and had not entirely separated from the Vedic religion like the later Śaiva sects), and the other three texts belong to the Śaiva canon which grew later under its inspiration. These four Tantric texts were authentic Śaiva-śāstras studied in India in the 7th and 8th centuries A.D. if not earlier, and Tumburu is definitely described in Yoga-Vāśiṣṭha Rāmāyaṇa as an aspect of Rudra. These texts were introduced in Kambuja for establishing the rites known as Devarāja, which, therefore, must represent a Śaiva cult. In the Sanskrit text of the inscription the cult is referred to as '*Siddhi*' called Devarāja, but it appears from other passages that Devarāja was a phallic representation of Śiva.[23] Thus the state-religion established in Kambuja by king Jayavarman II was a form of Tantrik Śaivism, which included some mystie rites and was based on the four Śaivaśāstras specified by name. That the king himself was a follower of the same religion can hardly be doubted. He is said in Ins. No. 89 to have performed ten millions (*koṭi*) of sacrifices.

22. *IHQ*. VI, p. 97.
23. See ante, f.n. (3) above.

Jayavarman's decision that the royal priest should be selected from the family of Śivakaivalya alone was also probably due to the strict adherence to the Śaiva *āgamas* according to which the Śivācāryas had to be chosen preferably from the Brahmanical families of North Indian origin. Such families with knowledge of Āgama-śāstras were probably rare in Kambuja and hence the choice was confined to a single family. Parallel instances may be quoted from India. The great Cola king Rājendra Cola is said to have appointed Sarvaśiva Paṇḍita Śivācārya as the priest of the Rājarājeśvara temple at Tanjore, and ordered that in future his *śiṣyas* and their *śiṣyas* alone belonging to the Āryadeśa, the Madhyadeśa and the Gauḍa-deśa shall be eligible for the office of chief priest. The Malla kings of Bhatgaon (Nepal) also had Brahmins from Bengal as their priests.[24] In any case there is hardly any doubt that the Kambuja Court was strongly influenced by Śaivism then prevailing in India.

Although there are few specific facts about Jayavarman II which can be said to be established beyond dispute, there is no doubt that Jayavarman II played an important rôle in the history of Kambuja. He delivered it from foreign yoke, first of Java and then of Champā, and gave the kingdom a unity and solidarity which it had lacked for a century. The Devarāja cult introduced by him remained the official religion for a long period. His final choice of the capital at Hariharālaya was destined to make the region of Angkor famous in the world on account of many grand palaces and temples built there by successive kings. All these explain the eminent position which Jayavarman occupied for centuries in the history of Kambuja, a fact testified to by most flattering references to him in a large number of later inscriptions. Most fulsome praise, for example, is bstowed on Jayavarman II in the Phnom Sandak Ins. (No. 69) of the time of Yaśovarman. After reference to his beauty and glory in the most extravagant phrases it adds a verse which has a double sense applicable both to the king and the grammarian Pāṇini, and extols the former's knowledge of the great grammar. Although such phrases generally do not mean much, their occurrence in an inscription long after his death undoubtedly indicates his power and popularity. Even now he is the divine hero of Kambuja which represents him as the son of Indra. The sacred sword of Kambuja, which is still used by the

24. *IHQ*, VI, p. 100.

Kambuja kings at the time of their coronation, and jealously guarded by priests who claim descent from the old Brāhmaṇas, is supposed to have been a relic of Jayavarman II who remains the national hero and a great landmark in Kambuja history.[25]

Jayavarman II died, as noted before, in 854 A.D. and received, after death, the name of Parameśvara. This kind of posthumous name was usually formed by adding the word *'loka'* or *'pada'* to a divine name (Brahmā, Viṣṇu, Śiva, Indra etc.). Almost all the successors of Jayavarman II possessed such names, but with one or two exceptions, such name is not associated with any predecessor of Jayavarman II.

After the death of Jayavarman II his son Jayavardhana ascended the throne under the name of Jayavarman (III). The inscription of Prasat Cak (No. 53) in the region of Angkor, which refers to the year 791 Ś (=809 A.D.) as the sixteenth year of his reign, mentions in detail a story of his hunting elephants. Other inscriptions also refer to his capturing elephants and one of them has even preserved the name of the chief of the royal elephant hunters. Except this inordinate passion for elephant hunting we do not know anything about him. He ruled from 854 to c. 877 A.D., and his posthumous name was Viṣṇuloka. With him ends the line of Jayavarman II.

According to the Chinese chronicle Man-Chu written in 863 A.D. the Khmer Empire extended in the north to Chen-nan of Nan-chao which most probably corresponded to the northern part of Alāvirāṣṭra, to the west of Tonkin.[26] As the author gathered his information by a personal visit to these regions in 862 A.D., we may regard it as true of the period of Jayavarman III. It would, therefore, follow that his kingdom included the whole of Laos in the north and almost touched the frontier of Yunnan. Of course it is impossible to say to what extent this is due to his own conquests. For it is likely that Jayavarman II not only united the whole of Kambuja but also added Laos to his dominions, and this would be quite in keeping with the traditional glory of Jayavarman II to which reference has been made above. In any case it is tolerably certain that under Jayavarman II or his son the Kambuja kingdom had developed into a powerful empire.

25. Maspero, p. 31.
26. Et. AS. II, p. 94.

This is corroborated by the Arab writers. Ya'kūbī, writing about 875 or 880 A.D., describes the Khmer kingdom as vast and powerful, the king of which receives homage of other kings.[27] Another Arab writer, Ibn Rosteh (903 A.D.), refers to the high standard of administration in the Khmer country. "There are", he says, "eighty judges. Even if a son of the king appears before them they would judge equitably and treat him as an ordinary complainant." We are further told by the same writer that "the principal revenue is derived from cock-fight which brings the king fifty *mans* of gold per day".[28] Masūdī, who wrote in 943, but evidently got his information from older writers as he repeats a great deal of their accounts, adds that the Khmer troops consist mainly of infantry because their country is full of hills and valleys, rather than plains and plateaus.[29]

Several Arab writers bestow high praises on the Khmers for their abstinence from wine and adultery (debauchery). Thus Ibn Khordādzbeh (844–848 A.D.) says: "The kings and peoples of India abstain from drinking of wine but they do not consider adultery as an illicit act, with the sole exception of the Khmer king who forbids both drinking and adultery".[30] This is repeated by Ibn Rosteh (903 A.D.) on the authority of an Arab traveller Abdullah Muhammad bin Ishak who lived in the Khmer country for two years. "During this period," says he, "I have never seen a king more opposed to sexual license and more severe against drinking, for he inflicts capital punishment for both the offences."[31] The same view is recorded by Abū Zayd (c. 916 A.D.).[32] But the kings had large harems. Ibn Al Fakīh (902 A.D.) says that the king maintains four thousand concubines.[33]

27. Ferrand-*Textes*, I. p. 48.
28. *Ibid*, pp. 71, 78.
29. *Ibid*, p. 93. The passage is, however, translated differently by Dr. S. M. H. Nainar in *Arab Geographers' knowledge of Southern India* (Univ. of Madras, 1942). According to him "the inhabitants mostly go on foot because their country is full of mountains and valleys, few plains and table lands" (p. 174).
30. Ferrand—*Textes*, I., p. 28.
31. *Ibid*, pp. 69-70.
32. *Ibid*, p. 85.
33. *Ibid*, p. 64.

Lecture V

THE RISE OF ANGKOR.

With the death of Jayavarman III ended the direct line of Jayavarman II, and one Indravarman ascended the throne in 799 S' (=877 A.D.) (Nos. 54, 89). He was very remotely related to the queen of Jayavarman II. For we learn from several inscriptions (Nos. 56, 60-2) that his father king Śrī Pṛthivīndravarman was the son of the maternal aunt of the queen of Jayavarman II, and his mother was the daughter of king Śrī Rudravarman and daughter's daughter of king Śri-Nṛpatīndravarman. King Rudravarman was also the maternal uncle of the queen of Jayavarman II. These relationships will be clear from the genealogical table given below:—

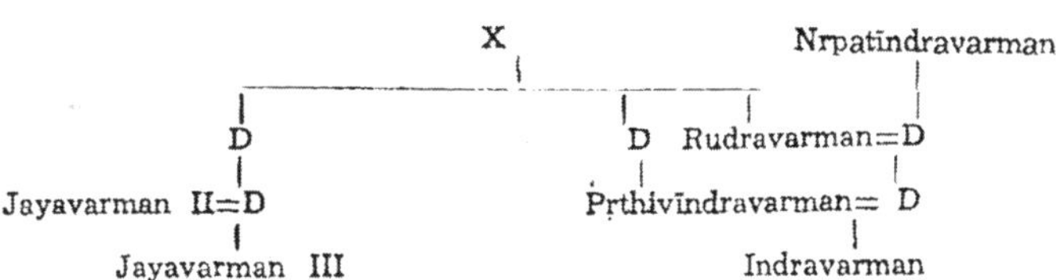

Where and when kings Nṛpatīndravarman, Rudravarman and Pṛthivīndravarman ruled it is difficult to say. They were either local chiefs ruling before Jayavarman II, or were vassals of the latter. In any case nothing is known of the reign of any of these three. It is difficult, therefore, to judge of the right of Indravarman to the throne of Kambuja, and we are ignorant of the circumstances under which he came to the throne.

It has been suggested that the marriage of Indravarman might have paved the way for his accession to the throne. According to the genealogical account of Yaśovarman (No. 60), Indradevī, the queen of Indravarman, was the daughter of king Mahīpativarman, and this Mahīpativarman was the son of Rājendravarman and his queen Nṛpatīndradevī. The same inscription informs us that Rājendravarman was connected with the royal family of Vyādhapura through his mother, and was a descendant of Puṣkarākṣa, who had united the kingdoms of Śambhupura and Aninditapura under his rule. The mother of Indradevī, named Rājendradevī, was descended from a royal family founded by Agastya a Brāhmana from Āryadeśa (i.e., India). These relationships, as well as the connection of Jayavarman II with these families, already explained above, will be clear from the following genealogical table

Nṛipatīndravarman (Ruler of Aninditapura)

Agastya (a Brāhmana from India) — Yaśomati (a royal princess) — Ruler of Vyādhapura — Puṣkarākṣa (also ruler of Śambhupura) — D | D

Narendravarman

Narendralakṣmī = Rājapativarman

D = S

Rājendravarman (= Nṛpatīndradevī) | Mahīpativarman

Jayavarman II (802-854 A.D.) | Jayavarman III (854-870 A.D.)

Rājendradevī = Mahīpativarman

Indradevī = Indravarman (acc. 877 A.D.)

This genealogy also does not give any clear or uncontestable right of succession to Indravarman through his queen, and raises the same doubt about the position of king Mahīpativarman and his predecessors *vis a vis* Jayavarman II and III. Here, again, we are forced to conclude that the royal ancestors of Indradevī were either local chiefs ruling before Jayavarman II or vassals of the latter and his son.

On the whole the genealogies of Indravarman and his queen seem to indicate that in addition to the two kingdoms of Śambhupura and Aninditapura there were other local kingdoms in Kambuja in the eighth century A.D., some of which probably continued as vassal states even during the reigns of Jayavarman II and Jayavarman III.

It is reasonable to conclude that Indravarman originally belonged to one of these states, and either the absence of any legitimate heir of Jayavarman III or some other circumstances, of which we have no knowledge, enabled him to secure the throne. It may be assumed that he did not rebel against the family of Jayavarman and come to the throne by violent means. For his inscriptions and those of his successors refer to Jayavarman II and III with respect and he appointed as his *guru* the grandson of the maternal uncle of Jayavarman II (No. 58).

It may be concluded from the epigraphic records that the whole of Cambodia had by this time been consolidated into a happy, rich and prosperous kingdom. Indravarman claims in his record (No. 58) that his commands were respectfully obeyed by the rulers of Cīna, Champā and Yavadvīpa. Such specific claims are not usually met with in the inscriptions of the Kambuja rulers and cannot be ignored as mere bombasts or figments of imagination. As regards Champā we have already noted that one of its generals advanced up to the heart of Kambuja and ravaged the kingdom early in the ninth century A.D. We may, therefore, presume that the struggle between the two kingdoms continued practically throughout the ninth century A.D. Indravarman's contemporary on the throne of Champā was a king bearing the same name who probably founded a new dynasty. We do not learn anything form the history of Champā which would either prove or disprove the claim of the Kambuja king. But we find about this time references to diplomatic missions from Champā to Java.[1] This latter must be the kingdom of Yavadvīpa mentioned by the Kambuja ruler as his vassal state. The diplomatic alliance between two states over both of which the Kambuja ruler claims supremacy may not be without significance. The reign of Indravarman coincides with an obscure period in Javanese history which saw the end of the kingdom of Matarām in Central Java and the shifting of the centre of political authority and Indo-Javanese culture to the eastern part of the island.[2] To what extent, if any, this final abandonment of Central Java was due to the rising power of Kambuja, we cannot say. But it is not unlikely that Kambuja, which suffered at the hands of both Champā and Java towards the close of the eighth and the beginning of the ninth century A.D., now turned against her old enemies and obtained some success. Unfortunately we have no definite knowledge of these events.

Indravarman's claim to supremacy over China is more puzzling, on the face of it, and will be discussed later.

Indravarman was a great builder. Ins. No. 54 (v. 7) informs us that immediately after ascending the throne he made a promise (*pratijñām kṛtavān*) that within five days counting from that very day, he would begin the work of construction (*prārapsye khananādikam*). The next verse tells us that he had constructed, according to his own design, a *siṁhāsana* (royal throne), the vehicle called Indrayāna, Indravimānaka, and Indraprāsādaka (probably two palaces), all made of gold (*haima*). He

1. *Champa*, p. 62.
2. *Suvarnadvipa*, I, pp. 237 ff.

installed three images of Śiva and three of the goddess (Durgā), which were works of his own art (*sva-śilpa-racitā*, v. 28). His various religious endowments, including temples and images of gods and a big tank called Indrataṭāka, are referred to in other inscriptions. His reign marks an important stage in the development of Kambuja art. Parmentier has made a special study of the monuments that may be definitely ascribed to Indravarman, and in his opinion, the art of Indravarman forms an intermediate stage between the Primitive and Classical art of Kambuja.

Indravarman ruled for only twelve years (877–889) and received the posthumous title Īśvaraloka. He was succeeded by his son Yaśovardhana under the name Yaśovarman. Yaśovarman occupies a place of honour in the history of Kambuja and his name has been immortalised by the foundation of a new capital city, on the top of the hill called Phnom Bakhen, which was at first called Kambupurī and later Yaśodharapura. Although this is not the famous city of Angkor Thom, covered with magnificent ruins, as was firmly believed until recent years, it extended round the hill and included a large part of the present site of Angkor Thom, and Yaśovarman may still be credited as the founder of Angkor, though in a qualified sense. The region round his newly founded capital city remained the heart of Kambuja power and culture till the last day of its greatness. He may be also said to have laid the foundation of the Angkor civilisation whose glory and splendour form the most brilliant chapter in the history of Kambuja.

Indravarman placed Vāmaśiva, the grand-nephew of Śivakaivalya, in charge of the education of Yaśovarman (No. 151 D. vv. 4–10). Yaśovarman is said to have been fond of Śāstras and Kāvyas (62 E.D. 1), and a perusal of his inscriptions leaves no doubt that Sanskrit literature, both secular and religious, was highly patronised in his court. These inscriptions are, however, poor in historical material. Reference is made to the numerous military campaigns of the king, including a naval expedition (62 D–B. 19), and he is said to have reinstated vanquished kings (62C–c. 5) and married their daughters (62C–B. 27). But they do not refer to specific events of his reign. The dominions over which Yaśovarman ruled were extensive. On the north it reached the frontiers of China, and on the west, the mountains which form the watershed between the rivers Menam and Salween. The eastern and southern boundaries were formed respectively by the kingdom of Champā and the sea.

King Yaśovarman has left numerous records (Nos. 60–73). Some of these refer to religious endowments and construction of sanctuaries while others give detailed regulations of the large number of monasteries founded by him.

The inscriptions of Yaśovarman are distinguished by two peculiarities. In the first place one single record (No. 60) is reproduced, in identical words, no less than eleven times. Secondly, the texts of these eleven inscriptions and of another (No. 61) are written twice, once in the ordinary alphabet used in Kambuja in those days, and again in a novel type of alphabet which has a close resemblance to the North Indian scripts. Further, seven inscriptions are written in this latter alphabet alone.[2a]

These inscriptions of Yaśovarman, in spite of vague generalities which they contain, give us many interesting sidelights on the various phases of his internal administration. They hold out a picture of a happy, prosperous and peaceful kingdom ruled over by an able and wise monarch who took all possible measures to ensure the welfare of the kingdom in all its aspects, political, economic, religious and social. The elaborate regulations framed by him give us an insight into the social and religious condition of the time and the earnest effort made by the king to improve it. Making all due allowances for exaggerations of court poets we must regard Yaśovarman as a brave general and ideal king, shining equally well in arts of war and peace. Himself a great scholar, he was a patron of art and science. He was liberal in his religious views, and although a devoted follower of Śaivism, he patronised Buddhism in an unstinted manner. He was a great king in every sense of the term. Perhaps the court poet did not exaggerate very much when he said that the glory of Yaśovarman was sung even after his death, by the people "in their games, on their beds, and in their travels" (No. 70). Yaśovarman received the very appropriate posthumous title of Paramaśivaloka.

Yaśovarman died about 908 A.D. The history of Kambuja during the next twenty years is somewhat obscure and uncertain. We know that two sons of Yaśovarman, *viz.* Harṣavarman I and Īśānavarman II ascended the throne one after another, and next came Jayavarman IV, the husband of the sister of Yaśovarman. But the known dates of these kings cannot be easily reconciled with

2a. Nos. 62 (A-E), 63A, 67.

a normal course of succession. The Sanskrit text of the Ins. No. 75 refers to a donation by king Harṣavarman, and the fragmentary Khmer text of the inscription contains the date 834 Śaka (=912 A.D.), but what connection, if any, this date has with the donation is not clear,[3] and we canr.ot therefore, say whether it falls during the reign of Harṣavarman. The Ins. No. 74 refers to Yaśovarman and his two sons and mentions a foundation made in 832 Śaka (=910 A.D.), but there is nothing in the context to show that this date falls within the reign of the last-named king viz. Īśānavarman II. The Ins. No. 78 is dated in 844 Śaka (=922 A.D.), in the reign of a king whose name begins with Ha, but as the next letter is not very legible, its restoration as Harṣavarman, though very probable, is by no means certain. The only konwn date of the sons of Yāśovarman is furnished by Ins. No. 98 which refers to an address (*nivedana*) presented to king Īśānavarman II in 847 S' (=925 A.D.). This certainly proves that Harṣavarman must have ceased to rule, and his younger brother Īśānavarman II ascended the throne some time before 925 A.D.

It is, however, difficult to reconcile this with the known dates of Jayavarman IV. Although Ins. No. 80 gives 928 A.D. as the date of his accession, we have actually one inscription (No. 76) dated in 921 A.D., belonging to his reign. What is more important, this inscription as well as two others (Nos. 77–77A), dated 921 A.D., found at Koh Ker, show that the tutelary deity of the Kambuja royal family was already transferred to that place, and consequently the capital city must have been removed there. This goes against the view, formerly held, that Jayavarman ruled as Viceroy at Koh Ker during the rule of Yaśovarman's son or sons. Finally the relationship between Jayavarman IV and his predecessors is not such as would induce us readily to believe that he had legitimate claim to the throne, and an expression in Ins. No. 84 (v. 2) implies that he came to the throne by his own might and not by any right of succession.

The most reasonable inference from the above facts seems to be that Jayavarman rebelled against Īśānavarman II and set up as an independent king even during his life-time, some time before 921 A.D., though in a later age, an attempt was made to obliterate the memory of the unpleasant incident by regarding his formal

3. Cf. *Corpus*, p. 552, f.n. 1.

accession to the throne to have taken place in 928 A.D., probably the year in which Īśānavarman II died.

Nothing more is known of Harṣavarman and Īśānavarman II, beyond the fact that their posthumous names were respectively Rudraloka and Parama-Rudraloka.

The most important event of the reign of Jayavarman IV was the removal of the capital to Koh Ker (Chok Gargyar) (No. 151). Evidently the new ruler did not like, or think it prudent, to remain at a city which was so intimately associated with the rulers whose throne he had usurped.

The choice of the new capital cannot be regarded as a happy one. It was situated in a wild barren country about 50 miles north-east of Angkor. Among the extant ruins we can still trace the remains of one principal and twelve subsidiary temples, and the usual artificial lake. A characteristic feature was a temple containing three huge monolithic *liṅgas* fashioned out of three natural boulders. This perhaps accounts for the fact that the town was not oriented as usual, its north-south axis being considerably inclined towards the west. Jayavarman also erected a pyramid more than 40 yards high, which was designed as the pedestal of the tutelary deity Devarāja.[5]

Jayavarman IV is described as having destroyed the ruler of Champā (No. 83A). This probably implies renewed hostilities with the eternal enemy on the eastern border, but we possess no detailed account of the struggle.

Jayavarman had the posthumous name of Paramaśivapada and was succeeded by his son Harṣavarman II. According to the generally accepted reading of the Ins. No. 85 the king ascended the throne in 864 S' (=942 A.D.). But the Ins. No. 84 belonging to his reign appears to be dated in 863 S' (=941 A.D.). As the other inscription is now lost and its reading cannot be checked, we cannot altogether dismiss the data supplied by the Ins. No. 84. The date of the accession of Harṣavarman II may, therefore, be earlier by at least one year than that generally accepted.[6] His posthumous name was Brahmaloka.

4. Cf. *BEFEO*. XXXI, pp. 12 ff.
5. *Inscriptions*, pp. 69-70.
6. *Ibid*, p. 261.

Harṣavarman II was suceeeded by Rājendravarman. Several inscriptions (Nos. 88, 89) refer to Rājendravarman as the elder brother of Harṣavarman II, and hence it has been generally held that Rājendravarman was the elder son of Jayavarman IV. Why the elder son reigned after the younger remained a mystery. This mystery was still more deepened by the Mebon Ins. (No. 89A) which says that Rājendravarman was the son of Mahendravarman and Mahendradevī. According to this inscription both Mahendravarman and his father ruled over a kingdom (the name of which except the last two syllables 'pura' has disappeared), and Mahendradevi was descended on the mother's side from Bālāditya, king of Aninditapura. Finot, who edited this inscription, tried to reconcile its data with the older view by suggesting that Mahendravarman was but another name of Jayavarman IV. Coedès however very properly rejected this hypothesis and offered an alternative view that Rājendravarman was the son of Mahendradevī by a previous husband Mahendravarman. All doubts have, however, been set at rest by the discovery of the Pre Rup Ins. (No. 93). We learn from it that Yaśovarman had two sisters Jayadevī and Mahendradevī. Jayadevī was married to Jayavarman IV and their son was Harṣavarman II. Mahendradevī was married to Mahendravarman and their son was Rājendravarman. Presumably Jayadevī was the elder sister, and hence her son Harṣavarman, although younger in age than Rājendravarman, had the prior right to succession. The Pre Rup Ins. further mentions Vedavatī, a descendant, by way of female line, of Sarasvatī, sister's daughter of Bālāditya who was descended from Kauṇḍinya and Somā. We are told that Mahendravarman was descended from the royal family of the father of Vedavatī while Mahendradevī was a descendant of Vedavatī herself. The genealogy may be explained by the following Table:

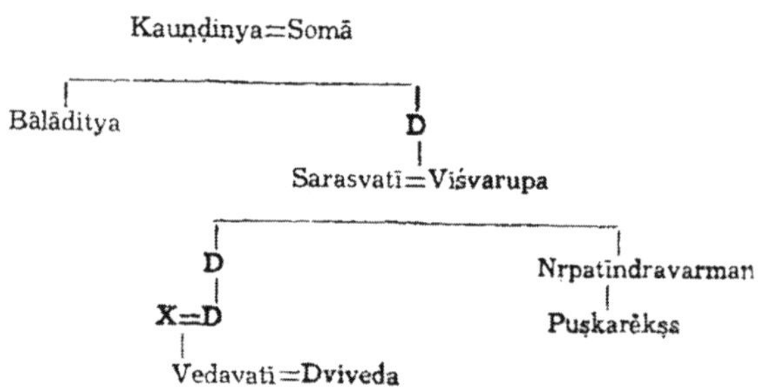

The succession after Yaśovarman may be shown by the following table:

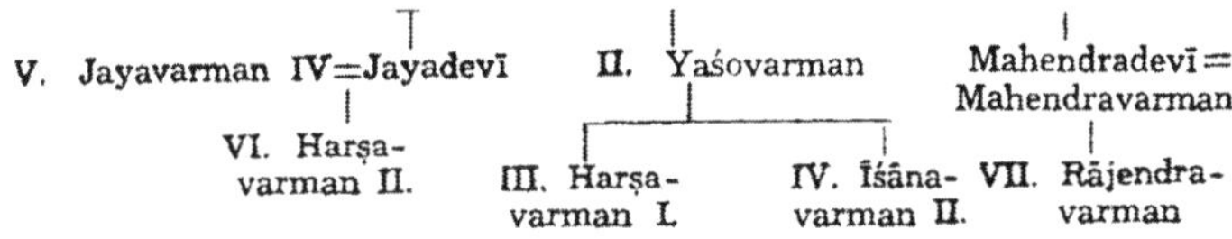

The succession of kings, marked by Roman numerals IV to VII, can only be regarded as natural and legitimate by supposing that Nos. III, IV, and VI left no issue at the time of their death. This is too unusual to be readily believed, and it is more likely that the whole period was marked by a struggle for succession among persons who were in some way connected with the royal family. We have already cited evidence which seems to corroborate this, at least in regard to Jayavarman IV.

Rājendravarman ascended the throne in 866 S' (=944 A.D.) at an early age (No. 93, vv. 27, 37, 52). The most important event in his reign is the removal of the capital back again to Yaśodhara-giri or Yaśodharapura, the city on the top of the Phnon Bakhen hill, founded by Yaśovarman. The Ins. No. 92 informs us that the king embellished the city which was deserted for a long time. There are some hints in the Ins. No. 93 that he had seized the royal power after some contest.[7] According to Aymonier the old Khmer story of prince Baksei (Skt. *pakṣī*=bird) Chan Krang refers to Rājendravarman.[8] That would, in effect, mean that his brother, the reigning king, was disturbed by a prophecy that the latter would be dethroned by him. Rājendravarman consequently had to fly for his life and ultimately defeated and killed his brother. Such a fratricidal struggle is not of course an improbable one, and that would at least satisfactorily explain the desertion of the capital associated with the family of his rival for two generations.

We possess a large number of very long *praśastis* of the reign of Rājendravarman but they do not throw much light on the political history of the period. Several inscriptions (Nos. 92, 93, 97) mention that he defeated the hostile kingdoms, particularly that of Champā.

7. *Ibid*, p. 75.
8. Aymonier I, p. 219.

Rājendravarman undoubtedly gained some success in his expedition against Champā. An Ins. from Champā informs us that the Kambujas had carried away the golden image of the Po Nagar Temple and the king of Champā had installed in its place a stone image in the year 887 (=965 A.D). Another Ins. in the same temple records the installation of the golden image of the goddess Bhagavatī in 840 (=918 A.D.), and the Kambuja invasion must have therefore taken place between these two dates. As the stone image was installed in 965 A.D., and such an important temple as that of Po Nagar was not likely to be left empty for a long time, the Kambuja invasion mentioned in the Po Nagar inscription probably refers to that of Rājendravarman. It would show that the Kambuja army advanced up to Khan Hoa province, and severely defeated the Chams.

Rājendravarman is also credited in his inscription (No. 93) with victorious campaigns in all directions, north, south, east and west, but no details are given, though as we shall see later, these may not be mere empty boasts.

Rājendravarman received the posthumous name of Śivaloka. He probably appointed his son Jayavarman as his regent in 968 A.D. and next year, on his death, the latter obtained full sovereignty.[9]

The reign of Jayavarman V was marked by a predominance of Buddhism as is clearly evidenced by the inscription (No. 106) engraved by his minister Kīrtipaṇḍita. It contains the instructions and regulations issued by the king for the propagation of Buddhist doctrines. But Śaivism remained the official religion.

Jayavarman also erected some notable monuments, such as Hemaśṛṅga-giri but its identification is uncertain.[10] He continued the aggressive policy against Champā and obtained some success (No. 114). He died in 1001 A.D. and his posthumous name was Paramvīraloka.

The period of a century and a quarter (877–1001 A.D.) covered by the reigns of Indravarman and his seven successors constitutes a landmark in the history of Kambuja, and it is necessary to emphasise some of the special features which characterise it.

9. *BEFEO*. XXVIII. p. 115.
10. *Ibid*, pp. 82-3.

In the first place, the period witnessed a great extension of the political power of Kambuja and therewith also the sphere of Indian culture and civilisation. This is proved by the Chinese annals which have fortunately preserved for us a fairly comprehensive picture of the political geography of Indo-China about the year 960 A.D. when the Song Dynasty began to rule in China. This, together with the information supplied by the chronicles of Burma and Siam, enables us to make a broad survey of the political condition of the whole of Indo-Chinese Peninsula lying to the south-east of India and south-west of China about the middle of the tenth century A.D.[11]

In the year 960 A.D. when Chao Kuang-in, the founder of the Song dynasty, seized the government of China, the whole of Tonkin with the districts of Than-hoa and Nghe-an lying to the south of it constituted the Chinese province of Ngan-nan. But the Chinese authority over this province was only nominal, for since the beginning of the tenth century A.D. it practically functioned as an independent state. In 968 A.D. the Chinese formally acknowledged its independence when its ruler Dinh Bo-linh proclaimed himself to be an Emperor and gave the new name Dai-co-viet to his kingdom.

To the north and north-west of this kingdom was the independent Hinduised Thai principality of Nan Chao (in N. Yunnan) that had freed itself from the Chinese yoke about 730 A.D. The Tang dynasty maintained a protracted struggle to re-establish its authority over this region, but failed. Indeed so painful was the memory of this fruitless campaign to the Chinese that when the general of the first Song Emperor proposed to his master to make another attempt to reconquer Nan Chao, the latter, reflecting upon the disasters sustained by the Chinese under the Tang dynasty, refused to have anything to do with it, and for the next three centuries Nan Chao remained an independent principality. With the loss of these two southern provinces the Chinese Emperor lost direct contact with the Indo-Chinese Peninsula.

To the south and west of these lay the three well-defined Hinduised kingdoms viz. Champā in the east, corresponding to Annam, Ramaṇṇadeśa in the west corresponding to lower Burma, and Kambuja in the south. The central region of the peninsula

11. For details, cf. *Et. As.* II. pp. 79 ff.

surrounded by these kingdoms was peopled by the Thais who had imbibed rudiments of Hindu civilisation. They set up a number of principalities which bore Hindu or Hinduised names, but it is not always easy to locate these kingdoms definitely.

The Kambuja inscriptions of this period, as we have seen above, refer to the conquest of China by some of its kings. The references are vague and general and, by themselves, do not enable us to form any definite idea of the nature and extent of the Kambuja power in respect of that mighty oriental kingdom. But it is evident from the Chinese annals that although Kambuja had nothing to do with the territory of China proper, it established its suzerainty over many states in the Indo-Chinese Peninsula which were formerly within the zone of the political supremacy of China, and this geographical expression in the Kambuja records must be construed accordingly.

As already noted above, the extension of Kambuja power in these northern regions can be traced as early as 863 A.D. But during the period under review the Kambuja sovereignty and Hindu culture seem to have been definitely established throughout the region up to the borders of the modern Chinese province Yunnan. The kingdom, which the Chinese call Nan-chao and is referred to as Mithilārāṣṭra in Thai chronicles, comprised the northern part of Yunnan. Immediately to its south lay the kingdom which is called Ālavirāṣṭra, the kingdom of the giant Ālavi. It comprised the southerh part of Yunnan. According to a contemporary Chinese chronicler, who visited these regions in 862 A.D., the northern part of Ālavirāṣṭra formed the boundary of the Khmer empire. When, therefore, Indravarman claims that his commands were obeyed by the king of China, and Yaśovarman asserts that his empire reached up to the frontier of China, we must presume a further expansion of the power of Kambuja at the cost of Mithilārāṣṭra (Chinese Nan-chao), which would extend the Kambuja power into the heart of Yunnan, probably not far from the border of the then kingdom of China. The memory of this Kambuja empire is preserved in the local annals. The chronicles of Yonaka which compirsed the two kingdoms of Ālavirāṣṭra and Haribhuñjaya record the foundation of Suvarnagrāma, the site of the later capital Xien Sen, by a Khmer emperor. The chronicle of Bayao, a town about 60 miles further south, on a branch of the upper Mekong river, states that ruins of old palaces and cities belonging to the old time of Khmer kings were scattered in mountains and forests when this city was founded. The victorious campaigns of Rājendravarman in all directions evidently relate to his campaigns in these regions. On the whole it may be safely presumed that throughout the reign of Indravarman's dynasty the Kambuja Empire extended in the north as far as Yunnan and included a considerable portion of it.

While the Kambuja kingdom was thus expanding along the valley of the Mekong river towards the north, it also extended its authority along the valley of the Menam on the west. In this region, which now constitutes the home provinces of the kingdom of Siam or Thailand, the country of Lavapuri, comprising all the territory between the Gulf of Siam in the south and Kampheng Phet on the north, formed a stronghold of Kambuja power. For a long time this was regarded as an integral part of the Kambuja kingdom. But the Kambuja kings also exercised political influence over the petty principalities of the local ruling chiefs that lay to its north. The successive kingdoms in this region in geographical order beginning from the south are Sukhodaya, Yonakarāṣṭra and Kṣmerarāṣṭra which touched the Kambuja kingdom of Alavirāṣṭra on the Mekong valley. The chronicles of these kingdoms refer to the Kambuja sovereignty over them and the very name Kṣmerarāṣṭra of the northernmost of these recalls the suzerainty of that people throughout the Menam valley. The Kambuja kings established a strongly fortified post at a place called Unmārgaśilānagara which commanded the roads to the upper valleys of both the Mekong and the Menam rivers, and although the petty vassal states on the Menam often revolted against the Kambuja authority, the Kambuja kings could always bring their forces from one region to the other through this road and subdue them. Many stories of such unsuccessful rebellions are preserved in the local annals.

The expansion of the Kambuja kingdom brought it into touch with the three important principalities in Burma which stood between it and the mainland of India. Ramaṇṇadeśa, the country of the Raman or the Mon as they are called today, comprising the whole of Lower Burma, Tavoy, Mergui and Tennasserim, was the most powerful of these three and was something like a federation of states such as Rāmāvati, Haṁsāvatī, Dvāravatī, Śrī Kṣetra, etc. The number of these states varied, but was never less than seven, all acknowledging the suzerainty of one of them which grew more powerful than the others from time to time. It was a strong centre of Hindu civilisation, and contained a large number of famous colonies of Indians. To its north lay the kingdom of Pagan or Arimardanapura, in Upper Burma, along the valley of the Irawaddy and the Chindwin. Still further to the north and north-east, along the valleys of the Upper Irawaddy and the Salween rivers lay a number of Thai States which were often federated together and designated as Kauśāmbī. The kingdom of Kambuja, occupying the central portion of Indo-Chinese peninsula, bordered all these three states which separated it from India. These regions have acquired a special importance in our days in view of the recent political situation. It is, therefore, interesting to note that they were never as remote and inaccessible from India as is generally supposed, and an unbroken series of Hindu or Hinduised kingdoms were spread over this vast area as far as the borders of China. Kambuja, the most powerful of all these states, not only established its political authority over the entire central part of this vast region but introduced the elements of Indian culture and civilisation among the primitive peoples, mostly belonging to the Thai race. It is evident from a study of the Thai chronicles that even those Thai peoples or principalities which did not acknowledge the political suzerainty of Kambuja copied its civilisation and gradually imbibed the different elements of Hindu culture, traces of which, both literary and monumental, are still scattered over the entire area. This is a fascinating chapter of Indian colonial history but the limits of our subject do not permit us to go into further details.

If we now turn from the north towards the south we find that Kambuja also came into contact with the mighty empire of the Śailendras in the Malay Peninsula. During the tenth century A.D. the northern part of this peninsula, lying, roughly speaking, to the north of the Isthmus of Kra, belonged to Kambuja, while the part to its south was included within the mighty empire of the Śailendras. We have no definite evidence of any political relation between the two, but Indravarman's claim of supremacy over Java may refer to a contest with the Śailendras who ruled over both Java and Malay Peninsula.

Although we are unable to find out the exact relationship between Kambuja and the Śailendras, we are in a better position as regards her eastern neighbour, the kingdom of Champā. It will appear from what has been said above that almost throughout the ninth and tenth century A.D. there were perpetual hostilities between Kambuja and Champā, and Kambuja scored some definits successes against Champā in the tenth century A.D.

This broad survey of the political condition of the Indo-Chinese Peninsula enables us to visualise how Kambuja grew to be a mighty power in Indo-China in the tenth century A.D. The history of the two succeeding centuries will show a further extent of its power and influance, but we must remember that the foundation of this future greatness was laid by the dynasty of Indravarman and mainly by the exertion of himself and such powerful kings as Yaśovarman and Rājendravarman. It is interesting to note in this connection that the Arab writer Ibn Al Fakih (902 A.D.) describes the Khmer kingdom as having an extent of 4 months' march.[12]

The second characteristic that marks the history of Kambuja during the tenth century A.D. is the intensification of Hindu culture. This may be clearly perceived from a study of the numerous inscriptions, more than fifty in number, that this period has bequeathed. Most of these inscriptions are written in Sanskrit, in beautiful and almost flawless Kāvya style, and some of them are quite big compositions. The text of an inscription of Yaśovarman (No. 60) of which we possess no less than eleven copies in different places contains fifty verses. Another (Nos. 62–63) with five copies contains 108 verses each. A third (No. 61) contains 93 verses of which only 15 are common with the last series. In addition to these there are a large number of records containing about fifty verses, a few more or less. But the *praśastis* of Rājendravarman exceed in size and quality even those of Yaśovarman. The Mebon Ins. of this king (No. 89A) contains 218 verses, not a few of which are fairly big, being written in Śārdūlavikrīḍita and Sragdharā metres. The largest inscription is that of Pre Rup (No. 93) which contains 298 verses. There are many other records of Rājendravarman and other kings of this period which run to a considerable length.

The authors of these inscriptions have very successfully used almost all the Sanskrit metres, and exhibit a thorough acquaintance with the most developed rules and conventions of Sanskrit rhetoric and prosody. Besides, they show an intimate knowledge of the Indian epics, Kāvyas and Purāṇas, and other branches of literature, and a deep penetrating insight into Indian philosophical and spiritual conceptions; they are also saturated with the religious and mythological conceptions of the different sects of India;—all this to an extent which may be justly regarded as marvellous in a community separated from India by thousands of miles. It is beyond the scope of this lecture to illustrate these by citing examples from the different inscriptions. But a verse may be quoted to show how

12. Ferrand-*Textes*, p. 64.

they were thoroughly conversant even with the grammatical treatise of Pāṇini: —

Rājanvatity=anya-nṛpo=nvaśāt prāṅ
Nipātanāl=lakṣaṇam=antareṇa |
Yo=lakṣaṇais=saṁskṛta-varṇṇavarddhi-
Padais=tu sādhutva-dharān dharitrīm | |
(No. 93, v. 48).

This verse is a pun on the rule of Pāṇini VIII 2·14 ('*rājanvān saurājye*). It makes an exception to the general rule about the elision of the final *n* before the consonant in the word *rājanvān* in the sense of 'having a good king', the ordinary form '*rājavān*' meaning only 'having a king'. There are similar references in an inscription of the time of Yaśovarman: —

Sad-dharma-nirater=yyasya pada-rājyena cakrire|
Upasarggāḥ kriyā-yoge te prāg dhātor=mmuner=iva | |
(No. 69, B. 13).

Here also the verse is a pun on Pāṇini's Sūtras 1,4,58,59,80 and compares king Jayavarman II with Pāṇini. Similarly v. 15 of Ins. 62A compares king Yaśovarman with Pāṇini and all the epithets are applicable to both. The Mahābhāṣya was studied, and according to an Ins. of Yaśovarman (No. 62D, D. 13) the king himself composed a commentary on it. The Minister of the king was an expert in Horāśāstra (No. 70, v. 8). Manu is mentioned as a legislator and a verse from Manu-smṛti is reproduced verbatim (62A, C, 8 and 9). Reference is also made to Vātsyāyana, as the author of Kāmasūtra (62D. D. 1), and Viśālākṣa as having composed a treatise on Nīti (62C, C. 15). The famous medical treatise of Suśruta is also mentioned in Ins. No. 61. (v. 49).

The Pre-Rup Ins. (No. 93) contains four verses definitely alluding to Kālidāsa's Raghuvaṁśa, repeating sometimes the very words used by the great poet. The inscriptions of Yaśovarman refer to Pravarasena (No. 62B, B. 7) and Mayūra (No. 62C, C. 16) as the authors, respectively, of Setubandha and Sūryaśataka, and to Guṇāḍhya (Nos. 62C, C. 15; 62D, B. 26) as a writer in Prākṛt with allusion to the legend about him contained in Kathāsarit-sāgara. The records frequently refer to the Trayī or Vedas, the Vedānta, Smṛti, the sacred canons of the Budhists and Jainas, and religious texts of various Brahmanical sects and schools of philosophy. As to the Puranic religion and mythology and legends contained in

Rāmāyaṇa, Mahābhārata and Harivaṁśa and the allusion, alliteration, simile, *etc.*, usually met with in Sanskrit literature, one will come across them at every step as he proceeds through these inscriptions.

These inscriptions bear ample testimony to the highly flourishing state of Sanskrit literature in Kambuja during this period. Unfortunately the Kambuja inscriptions are not generally known or studied in India. Otherwise they would have long ago been recognised as constituting an important addition to the Sanskrit Kāvya literature of ancient India. It may be said without any hesitation that like the Kambuja monuments the Kambuja Sanskrit records on stone far exceed in volume and grandeur those of ancient India of which the existence is so far known. This is no mean compliment to the culture that the sons and daughters of India developed on the distant soil of Kambuja and spread far into the interior across the hills and dales of Laos and other inaccessible regions of the Indo-Chinese Peninsula.

But apart from their literary merit these inscriptions are invaluable as testifying to the thoroughness with which Indian culture and civilisation, in all its aspects, was imbibed in Kambuja. This is particularly applicable to the religious and spiritual life. The inscriptions give evidence of the minute knowledge of the rules, regulations and practices of religion, particularly of the Śaiva and Vaiṣṇava sects, and show a thorough acquaintance not only with the various gods and goddesses in their numerous names and forms but also with the philosophical conceptions lying behind them. The prominent place occupied by religion in the life of the people is also demonstrated by the large number of temples and images erected and installed by kings and others. Most of the inscriptions refer to these pious foundations, and ruins of many of them are now lying scattered all over the country. But what strikes one more is that we find in Kambuja not only the external forms of Indian religion but that ethical and spiritual view of life which was the most distinguishing feature of ancient Indian civilisation. Anyone who carefully studies the inscriptions of Kambuja cannot fail to be struck with the spirit of piety and renunciation, a deep yearning for emancipation from the trammels of birth and evils of the world, and a longing for the attainment of the highest bliss by union with Brahma, which formed the keynote of their life and is expressed with beauty and elegance in language at once sombre and serene.

Even the kings, high officials and the nobility of the kingdom were inspired by these high ideals. One of the interesting characteristics of the Kambuja court-life is the very intimate association between the secular and spiritual heads. The kings received their instruction in early life from eminent religious *ācāryas* and there are many instances where sons of kings and members of the royal family became High Priests and Ācāryas. The inter-marriage between the royal and priestly families was also a matter of frequent occurrence. The predominance of the priestly families who supplied royal priests for successive generations, such as we find in the Sdok Kak Thom Inscription, already referred to above, is both an index and a cause of the spiritual outlook of the king and the people. The tutelary deity of the kingdom with the cult of Devarāja, placed in charge of a long line of High Priests who were the *gurus* or preceptors of the kings, must have helped to a great extent in moulding the whole view of life in the kingdom.

But while all these causes undoubtedly operated in developing the religious and spiritual life of the people, its main source must have been a close, constant and intimate contact with India. Fortunately this is not merely a hypothesis but may be proved by definite examples recorded in inscriptions of Kambuja. Rājalakṣmī, the daughter of Rājendravarman, and the younger sister of Jayavarman, was married to an Indian Brāhmaṇa Divākara Bhaṭṭa who was born on the bank of the river Kālindī or Yamunā sacred with the association of Kṛṣṇa's boyhood (No. 103). One of the ancestors of Yāśovarman's mother, Agastya, is said to be a Brāhmaṇa of Āryadeśa versed in Vedas and Vedāṅgas (Nos. 60–62). Another Brāhmaṇa named Sarvajñamuni, versed in the four Vedas and all the āgamas, and devoted to Śiva, was born in Āryadeśa (No. 170) He came to Kambudeśa and his descendants occupied high religious office. There are many other less specific references to such migrations.[13] There is also evidence that the learned Brāhmanas of Kambuja visited India. The most important instance is that of Śivasoma, the *guru* of Indravarman. We learn from an inscription (No. 58) that Śivasoma was the grandson of king Śrī Jayendrādhipativarman, maternal uncle of Jayavarman II, and that he learnt the *Śāstras* from Bhagavat-Śaṅkara whose lotus feet were touched by the heads of all the sages. It has been rightly conjectured by

13. Ins. No. 161 probably refers to such a case. A learned *muni* was brought from a foreign land, which is not specified, in a fleet of barges.

the editor of the Ins., that the reference here is undoubtedly to the famous Śaṅkarācārya,[13a] and presumably Śivasoma must have come to India to sit at the feet of the venerable Śaṅkara. It may be noted in passing that as Indravarman lived towards the close of the ninth century A.D. Śivasoma must have flourished about the middle of the ninth century A.D., which agrees with the date generally assumed for Śaṅkarācārya.

The visit of Kambuja scholars to India may also be presumed on indirect evidence. M. Coedès, while editing the Vat Thipedi Ins. (No. 73), has pointed out that it exhibits all the characteristics of the Gauḍa style, described by Sanskrit rhetoricians, in such a striking manner, that its author must have either been born in Gauḍa or lived in that region.

Though we can cite only a few actual instances of the learned Brāhmaṇas of India, versed in sacred scriptures, settling in Kambujadeśa, and the learned priests of the latter country visiting India, they corroborate what may be regarded as the only reasonable hypothesis that offers a satisfactory explanation of the thoroughness with which literary, religious and spiritual culture of India was imbibed by the people of Kambuja.

It appears from the Kambuja inscriptions that the centres of Indian culture in Kambuja, from which it radiated all over the country, were the large number of *āśramas* which were founded by royal munificence and private efforts. Reference has already been made to these *āśramas* and the regulations concerning them in connection with king Jayavarman III. But they were very much developed during the period under review. According to Ins. No. 61 king Yāśovarman founded one hundred excellent *āśramas* in all parts of the kingdom. In spite of the possible exaggeration in number, there is no doubt that the king founded quite a large number of institutions of this kind. For the twelve diagraphic inscriptions (Nos. 60–61) undoubtedly refer to these *āśramas*, called after the king Yaśodharāśrama, each being situated in a different locality and associated with a local temple containing a

13a. Mr. S. Srikantha Sastri M.A. has opposed this identification, on grounds which appear to be very weak (*IHQ*. Vol. XVIII, pp. 175 ff). For arguments in favour of the identification cf. my paper in *Indian Review* (February, 1940) and an article by Prof. K. A. Nilakanta Sastri (*JOR*. Vol. XI, pp. 3-4).

deity whose name is mentioned. Barring the passage containing the name of this divinity, the inscriptions are identical, and their most interesting part is that which contains elaborate regulations for these *āśramas*, from which we quote the following extract.

"All the things, which the king Yaśovarman has given to the Āśrama (Yāśodharāśrama)—pearls, gold, silver, cows, horses, buffaloes, elephants, men, women, gardens etc., are not to be taken away by the king or anybody else. Into the interior of the royal cella—the king, the Brāhmans and the offspring of kings (kṣatriyas) can alone enter without taking off their ornaments. Others, such as the common people forming the escort of nobles, can only enter in a humble dress without garlands—the flower *nandyāvarta* however being allowed in their case too. (The common people) should not take any food or chew the betelnut there. The common people (not forming the escort of nobles) will not enter. There should be no quarrels. (Mock) ascetics of bad character should not lie down there. Brahmans, worshippers of Śiva and Viṣṇu, good people of good manners, can lie down there to recite their prayers in a low voice and to give themselves up to meditation. With the exception of the king—whoever passes in front of the monastery shall get down from his chariot and walk uncovered by an umbrella. This is not applicable to strangers. The excellent ascetic, who is appointed the head of the monastery, should always offer food, drink, betel and do all the duties, as for example offering welcome to guests, such as Brāhmans, children of kings (ksatriyas), ministers, the leaders of the army, ascetics of the Śaiva and Vaiṣṇava cult, and the best among the common people. They are to be honoured according to the order laid down here".[14]

As will be evident from these regulations, the *āśramas* to which they applied were open to all sects and classes of people. But three other inscriptions refer to *āśramas* specially meant for Vaiṣṇavas, Śaivas and Buddhists (Nos. 62A, 63, 63A). These were called respectively Vaiṣṇavāśrama, Brāhmaṇāśrama, and Saugatāśrama. The second name is somewhat puzzling, for in the regulations quoted above the term Brāhmaṇa appears as a general designation of a caste and there is nothing to indicate that it specifically refers to the Śaivas alone. The regulations concerning these sectarian *āśramas* are more detailed, and although there is much in common,

14. The English translation is quoted from Chatterji—pp. 115-116. I have substituted 'royal cella' for 'royal hut' in translating '*rāja-kuṭi*'.

there are some differences due to the emphasis laid on the special characteristics of the three religious sects.

These *āśramas* were in charge of a *Kulādhyakṣa*—corresponding to the *Kulapati* of the previous ones—and it is laid down at the beginning that he and his assistants (*karmakara*) must observe the regulations (*śāsana*) laid down for the particular *āśrama*. His first duty is to honour the guests and show all kinds of hospitality to them. If the king comes there with the ladies of his harem he shall entertain them as gods with all the resources at his command. For, as laid down by Vyāsa, the king is the supreme lord of the earth and the *guru* of the entire world, and whatever he wishes must be done. Next to the king, the Brāhmaṇas shall be honoured above others, and if there is more than one, the preference will be shown according to their character (*śīla*), qualification (*guṇa*) and learning. Then he should honour in order of precedence, prince, minister, military chief and good men. Special honour should be shown to the hero (*śūra*) who has displayed bravery in battle. One who loves to fight shall be preferred to one who avoids it, for the defence of *dharma* depends on the former.

As to the persons next in order of precedence the regulations differ. In the case of Vaiṣṇavāśramas, first come those who know the three Vedas, and then the *ācāryas* versed in grammar, preference among the persons of the same category being given to one who observes *brahmacarya*. Further, in preference to those who know the Pāñcarātra or the grammar, honour should be shown to the teachers of these two sciences.

In the Brāhmaṇāśrama, on the other hand, first the Brāhmaṇas and then the Śaiva and Pāśupata *ācāryas* should be honoured, preference among them being given to the one who knows grammar. One who teaches Śaiva and Pāśupata doctrine or grammar is to be preferred to those who are versed in them. In the Saugatāśrama, too, the learned Brāhmaṇa should be honoured a little more than the *ācārya* versed in Buddhist doctrine or in grammar, he who knows both being preferred to the other. The teacher of Buddhist doctrine or grammar should be preferred to one who merely knows these subjects.

Next in order of precedence in all the three *āśramas* is the learned *gṛhastha*, for learning is the best of the qualifications. Wealth, family, age, pious work and learning are the five titles of respect, each being superior to the one preceding it—this is evidently a quotation from Manu II. 136.

The Royal Decree then proceeds to say that the *Kulādhyakṣa* shall give food, medicine and other necessaries to common people, particularly the boys, old men, poor, destitute and those suffering from illness, and worship the calf *kapilā* by offer of grass etc.

The *Kulādhyakṣa* shall also offer balls of rice and perform *tarpaṇa* (funeral offering) at the *parvan* day, at the time of eclipse or at the end of each month, to the departed souls of those who were devoted or fell fighting or of those children, old men, poor and destitute, who had no relations to offer *piṇḍa*.

Those engaged in study in the āśramas,–Vaiṣṇavas, Brāhmaṇas, or the Buddhist Bhikkhus, as the case may be,—shall be supplied their daily necessaries, minute details of which are laid down with great care.

If any innocent man seeks refuge in the *āśramas* out of fear, he shall not be surrendered, and no one shall do any injury to another by words, thought or deed. Inoffensive animals shall not be killed within the boundaries of the *āśrama*.

The daughter and grand-daughter of the king, old ladies of the royal family and the chaste women shall be honoured as guests, but they must not enter the monastic cells. Women of bad character shall not be permitted to enter even if they offer themselves as guests. In addition there is a rule in the case of the Buddhist and Vaiṣṇava *āśrama* alone, that no inmate shall have any dealing with any woman, even though she may be his wife or co-religionist (*saha-dharmacārī*), within the environs of the *āśrama*.

The regulations conclude with a list of officers and servants, specifying the service to which an *adhyāpaka* or *kulapati* is entitled from them. Among the employees are two scribes, two keepers of books, and six men who prepared the leaves of manuscripts (*patrakāraka*), showing that each *āśrama* was provided with a library (*pustakāśrama*) to which reference is made in other inscriptions.

I have referred to these *āśrama* regulations at some length, for they reveal a picture of the social and religious life of Kambuja, such as we cannot get anywhere else. These *āśramas* were quite large in number, and spread over the whole country, and they served as strongholds or citadels of the Hindu culture and civilisation in its progress of conquest over the primitive culture of the land.

There is one singular circumstance in connection with the inscriptions setting forth these regulations. Some of them are digraphic i.e., their texts are written in the normal Kambuja alphabet and again repeated in the North-Indian alphabet current at that time. Some of the texts are written in this latter script alone. No satisfactory explanation of this somewhat unusual feature has been forthcoming. It is reasonable to suppose that the text was written in North-Indian alphabet for the convenience of those who recently arrived from India and were not yet familiar with the Kambuja alphabet. They might have been pilgrims or ascetics who went there for short or long periods, if not for permanent settlement. For, regular or periodical visits of Indian religious teachers to Kambuja appear very likely. According to this hypothesis the digraphic inscriptions would be very strong evidence of an intimate relation between India and Kambuja.

Lecture VI

THE KAMBUJA EMPIRE

The death of Jayavarman V was followed by disputed succession and civil war lasting for nearly ten years. The events that followed one another cannot be determined with absolute certainty, but the inscriptions discovered so far enable us to form a general idea of the situation.[1]

The immediate successor of Jayavarman V was Udayādityavarman I who ascended the throne in 923 Ś (=1001 A.D.). The Ins. No. 117, dated in that year, gives a genealogy from which it appears that Udayādityavarman's mother, descended from the family of Śreṣṭhapura, was the elder sister of the queen of Jayavarman V, and had an elder brother named Rājapativarman who was the *senāpati* of the same king. This relationship is not such as would make us believe, without further evidence, that the succession was legitimate. That it was not peaceful is clear from the fact that we have another king Sūryavarman who issued inscriptions in the self-same year 923 Ś (1001 A.D.) (No. 126).[2] To make the matter worse still, we find a third king Jayavīravarman issuing inscriptions in the year 925 Ś (=1003 A.D.) (No. 122). As a matter of fact Udayādityavarman I disappears from the scene altogether, under circumstances not known to us, from 1002 A.D. leaving the field to the two adversaries Sūryavarman I and Jayavīravarman. Sūryavarman I ultimately came out victorious, but we have records of Jayavīravarman from 925 to 928 Ś (=1003 to 1006) (No. 132). An analysis of the findspots of the inscriptions of these two kings shows that Jayavīravarman ruled in Angkor region and the regions to the west, while Sūryavarman ruled in the north-eastern regions. An inscription found at Tuol Don Srei (No. 129) says of Sūryavarman I that he carried on a war for 9 years and obtained the royalty in 924 Ś (=1002 A.D.). The date 924, as that of his accession, is also given in many other records.[3] Now, it can hardly be accepted that the nine

1. Cf. *BEFEO*. XXXIV, pp. 420 ff.
2. Cf. also Ins. No. 117, v. 6.
3. Nos. 148, 149.

years' war preceded his accession, for in that case the war would have begun eight years before the death of Jayavarman V, whose reign appears from all accounts to be a peaceful one. The probability, rather, is that the nine years' war refers to the struggle between Sūryavarman and Jayavīravarman at the end of which, i.e. about 932 Ś, the former finally triumphed over his rival and enjoyed the undisputed monarchy of Kambuja. Why the year 924 was chosen later as the formal date of his accession, although his reign began at least one year earlier in 923, it is difficult to say. Possibly Udayādityavarman died in 924 (1002 A.D.), and Sūryavarman, who later tried to establish his claim to the throne by his relationship with previous kings, tried to pass himself as the legitimate successor of Udayāditya after his death.

Nothing is known of the antecedents of Jayavīravarman. The inscriptions of Sūryavarman also refer to his origin in a somewhat vague manner. Ins. No. 148 says that he was born in the family of Indravarman. Ins. No. 146 repeats the same thing and adds that his queen Śrī Vīralakṣmī was born of the royal line of Śrī Harṣavarman and Śrī Īśānavarman. This is corroborated by No. 144. On the other hand Ins. No. 74B connects him with the maternal family of Indravarman. The Ins. No. 158 also probably refers to Sūryavarman as descended from the maternal family of Jayavarman V, but as some words of the verse are missing, one cannot be sure of the interpretation.[4] In any case these references show that Sūryavarman had no legitimate claim to the throne by his relationship with any of his immediate predecessors, though he and his queen probably belonged to aristocratic families which claimed some relationship, however remote, with the royal family of Indravarman. The theory that Sūryavarman originated from a ruling family in Siam or Malay Peninsula is an ingenious conjecture but lacks convincing proof.[5] According to Ins. No. 149

4. Cf. *Corpus*, p. 136, f.n. 4.

5. The view was propounded by Coedès on the basis of a statement in *Camadevivaṁsa* (a Pāli chronicle) to the effect that the king of Kambuja, son of the king of Siridhammanagara, attacked Haripuñjaya, about 20 years before the emigration of its inhabitants to Sudhammapura. As this event took place about 1056-7 A.D., the king of Kambuja must be Sūryavarman. As Siridhammanagara is Ligor in the Malay Peninsula, it would follow that Sūryavarman was a Malay prince. Coedès further points out that the title *Kaṁtvan*, introduced by Sūryavarman, is derived from Malay *tuan*, a chief. This assumption also explains Sūryavarman's leanings towards Buddhiam,

(v. 7) Sūryavarman gained the kingdom by fighting with and defeating its ruler, who was surrounded by other kings or in a state of intoxication.[6] This fully corroborates what we have said above. The same inscription refers to the king as being versed in Bhāṣyas, Kāvya, six Darśanas and Dharmaśāstras.

This scholarly king seems to have been a Buddhist; for his inscription (No. 149) contains invocation to Buddha along with that to Śiva, and his posthumous name was Nirvāṇapada. He issued edicts containing regulations about monasteries in which it was laid down that the ascetics and the Buddhist monks should offer to the king the merits of their piety (No. 139). But although he might have adopted the Buddhist faith, he did not give up the royal tutelary deity, and constructed both Śaiva and Vaiṣṇava temples. He is also said to have established the caste-system.[7]

There is no doubt that there was a prolonged civil war in Kambuja during the early part of his reign which probably continued till 1010 A.D. As a safeguard against similar outbreaks in future the king instituted a novel system which is known from ten inscriptions (No. 136), all dated 1011 A.D., eight of which are engraved on the pillars of the gopuram leading to the inner court of the royal palace of Angkor Thom, and two on gateways of a neighbouring building. They contain the text of an oath, and the names of district officers, numbering more than four thousand, who took it in the presence of the sacred fire and the Brāhmaṇas and the *ācāryas*, offering unswerving and lifelong homage and allegiance to the king, and dedicating their lives to his service.[8]

Some of the expressions are very interesting. The officers swore that they "shall not honour any other king, shall never be

indicated by his posthumous title Nirvāṇapada, for Ligor was a stronghold of Buddhism (*BEFEO*. XXV. pp. 24-5). This view, however, does not agree very well with the deduction made above from the findspots of inscriptions, *viz*., that Sūryavarman was at first ruler in the north-east, while his rival, Jayavīravarman ruled over the western part of Kambuja, which is adjacent to Siam and Malay Peninsula.

6. The meaning of the expression '*rāja-saṁkirṇna*' is however very doubtful.

7. No. 148, B. 8. The expression is '*varṇnabhdge kṛte*'. But as caste system is referred to in earlier records we cannot take the expression to mean that he introduced it for the first time. Possibly he re-organised it.

8. Almost identical oath is taken by the royal officials of Cambodia even today on the occasion of the royal coronation (*BEFEO*. XIII. 6, p. 16, and f.n. 3).

hostile (to their king) and shall not be the accomplices of any enemy." These seem to refer to the recent civil war between Sūryavarman and Jayavīravarman, though the inscriptions add that Sūryavarmadeva has been in complete enjoyment of the sovereignty since 924 Ś (=1002 A.D.). Sūryavarman seems to have conquered the whole of Siam, and even carried his victorious campaign to the Mon Kingdom of Thaton in Lower Burma. But unfortunately no details are known.[8a]

Sūryavarman was succeeded in A. D. 1049 by Udayādityavarman II, who is said to have been born in a royal family. We do not know definitely whether Udayāditya was the son of Sūryavarman. According to the Lovek Ins. (No. 158) "when Sūryavarman went to heaven, Udayādityavarman was crowned emperor (*cakravartī*) by his ministers." This rather implies that he owed the throne, not to rights of legitimate succession, but to the influence of a party in the court. That perhaps explains the series of revolutions that harassed him throughout his reign. A graphic description of three rebellious outbreaks is given in right epic style in the Prah Nok Ins. (No. 153) which commemorates the valour and heroism of the general Saṅgrāma who, being appointed the commander-in-chief for the protection of Rājalakṣmī (royal fortune), stood by his king and defeated the rebels.

The standard of revolt was raised in 1015 A.D. by Aravindahrada who made himself master of the southern half of the kingdom (v. 11). It is very likely that Aravinda was really a rival claimant to the throne, and contested it immediately after the death of Sūryavarman; but being foiled in his efforts by the court-party he set up as an independent king in the south. In any case even the record of his enemy pays tribute to his military skill and the equipment of his army, and we are told that several distinguished generals sent against him proved unsuccessful. At last Saṅgrāma asked for and obtained the permission of the king to lead the expedition against the rebel. Saṅgrāma defeated the rebel who fled to Champā.

The second rebellion was led by a favourite general of the king named Kamvau. Having collected a strong force, he overran the kingdom and defeated the royal army sent against him, after

8a. This information is contained in Mon Annals (*JBRS*. XII, pp. 39 ff.; BEFEO. XXV, p. 24. 24).

killing several renowned generals. At last Saṅgrāma went in person to meet this dreaded foe. In the sanguinary battle that followed, the two rival generals faced each other and Kamvau first struck Saṅgrāma with an arrow. Saṅgrāma, unperturbed, replied by shooting three arrows which pierced the head, the neck and the breast of Kamvau (v. 48). He fell down and died, and his army was routed.

The third rebellion was led by a chief called Slvat, who was aided by his yonger brother Siddhikāra and another hero named Sagāntibhuvana, each of whom prided himself as surpassing Kamvau in valour. But once more the general Saṅgrāma defeated them and the rebel army took to flight. Saṅgrāma pursued them as far as Praśānvrairmmyat but had to stop there to defeat some powerful enemy of the locality. After defeating him he again continued his pursuit of the rebel army of Slvat, and having bound the enemies in chains presented them to his royal master. He was richly rewarded by the grateful king for his unparalleled devotion and loyalty.

This third rebellion was quelled in or about the year 1066 A.D. i.e. towards the very end of the king's reign. Thus practically the whole life of the king passed in great troubles. An echo of these troubles is reflected in several inscriptions. The Prasat Prah Khset Ins. (No. 154), for example, refers to the restoration of a *liṅga* that was damaged by the enemy Kamvau. This inscription also mentions a relation of king Udayārkavarman well-known in Madhyadeśa. Udayārkavarman is no doubt the same as Udayādityavarman, but if Madhyadeśa denotes the well-known region in India, it would follow that the king was connected with India.

According to the Prasat Sralau Ins. (No. 156) the king deserted the town of Vrah Damnap. This is also evidently due to the troublesome rebellions. Udayāditya seems also to have sustained reverses in his wars against Champā.[9] Two inscriptions of Champā, dated 1050 A.D., refer to the glory of its king Jaya Parameśvaravarmadeva as having penetrated into the Kambu kingdom. Another inscription dated 1056 A.D. says that the king's nephew and general Yuvarāja Mahāsenāpati defeated the Khmers, took the town of Śambhupura and destroyed all its sanctuaries. The details of this campaign and the cause of the war are not known. The kingdom of Champā at the beginning of the reign of Udayā-

9. *Champa* pp. 146, 148-9, 155.

ditya was passing through a series of troubles and considerably weakened by the recent Annamite invasions. It is not impossible, therefore, that the Kambuja king took the aggressive. But it appears that he sustained serious reverses as the Cham army advanced up to the Mekong and pillaged the town of Śambhupura.

The Sdok Kak Thom Inscription (No. 151), which records the glory of generations of royal priests from the time of Jayavarman II, was engraved during the reign of Udyādityavarman II. It thus covers a period of two centuries and a half (802-1052) during which the same family supplied the high priests for the worship of the Royal God Devarāja. Jayendrapaṇḍita of this family was the *guru* of Udayādityavarman II, and taught him astronomy, mathematics, grammar, Dharmaśāstra, and all the other Śāstras.

The king had also another guru named Saṅkarapaṇḍita. The Lovek Ins. (No. 158) tells us that in imitation of the golden mountain of Jambudvīpa where dwell the gods, he had a golden mountain built in the city, and consecrated a Śiva-liṅga in a golden temple on the summit of the mountain.[10] Śaṅkarapaṇḍita was appointed a priest of this liṅga, and apparently wielded a great influence in the state. For we are told that when Udayādityavarman II died, Śaṅkarapaṇḍita, along with the ministers, placed his younger brother (by the same mother) Harṣavarman on the throne, and performed the ceremony of royal consecration. Śaṅkarapaṇḍita, of course, continued as royal priest. At the conclusion of the Lovek Ins. recorded by him, we are told that he was born, on the mother's side, in the family called *Saptadevakula*, and served three kings as priests. This implies that he was also the priest of Sūryavarman.

Harṣavarman III ascended the throne in A.D. 1066.[11] The most important events of his reign are his expeditions to Annam. In 1076 A.D. the Chinese emperor having decided upon an expedition against Annam, invited the rulers of Champā and Kambuja to

10. This has been identified by P. Stern with the central tower of Bayon, but Coedès identifies it with Baphuon (*BEFEO*. XXXI. 18 ff.; XXVIII, 81 ff).

11. Ins. No. 156 gives the date 987 S' (=1065 A.D.) for Harṣavarman III, but according to Nos. 153 and 154 Udayādityavarman II was reigning in 988 S'. This apparent contradiction can be solved by supposing either (1) that the dates in the last two are current, and that in the first, an expired year, or (2) that Harṣavarman III was proclaimed king during the lifetime of his brother, or (3) that one of the dates is wrong. The first alternative seems to be preferable (cf. *Inscriptions*, p. 222).

help him. They sent military expeditions which retreated after the defeat of the Chinese.[12] Not long after this, hostility broke out between the kings of Kambuja and Champā. The details of the campaign are briefly referred to in the Cham inscriptions as follows: "Harivarma (IV) (king of Champā) defeated the troops of Kambuja at Someśvara and captured the prince Śrī Nandanavarmadeva who commanded the army." The battle must have taken place some time before 1080 A.D.[12a]

The foreign expeditions ending in defeat and disaster must have considerably weakened the power and prestige of the king and probably led to a political disintegration of the Kambuja kingdom. For although Harṣavarman III continued to rule till at least 1089 A.D. (No. 159), we find another king Jayavarman (VI) issuing inscription in 1082 A.D. (No. 160). There is hardly any doubt, therefore, that towards the close of the eleventh century A.D., if not earlier still, during the troublesome reign of Udayādityavarman II, there were at least two rival kings in Kambuja. From an analysis of the findspots of inscriptions, so far discovered, it would appear that while Harṣavarman III ruled in the Angkor region and to its south, Jayavarman VI ruled in the north and north-east.[13] This state of things probably continued till Sūryavarman II, the second successor of Jayavarman VI, once more reunited the whole kingdom under his authority.

Jayavarman VI does not appear to have been related in any way to his predecessors. The following genealogy of his family, whose ancestral home was Mahīdharapura,[13a] is furnished by the inscriptions Nos. 172 and 177.

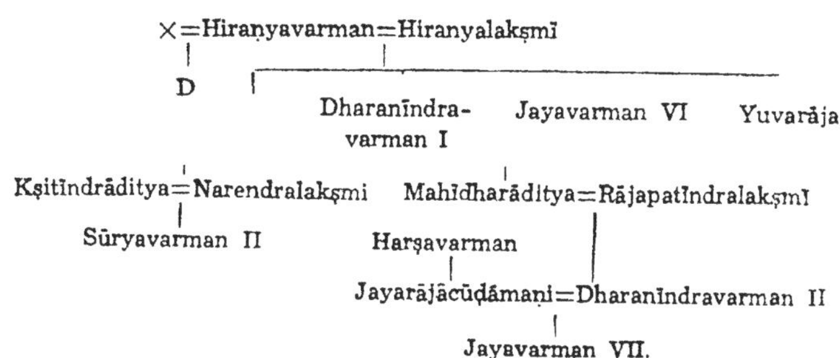

12. *BEFEO*. XVIII, No. 3, p. 33.
12a. *Champa*, p. 165.
13. *BEFEO*. XXIX. 299-300.
13a. For a critical account of the dynasty of Mahīdharapura cf, *BEFEO*. XXIX, p. 297.

Hiraṇyavarman is called *nṛpa*, *mahīpati* and *janeśa*, but whether he was an independent king or a vassal under Harṣavarman or his predecessor is difficult to say. The fact that Jayavarman VI became king before his elder brother seems to show that in his case there was no question of a legitimate succession to the hereditary kingdom, but acquisition of royal authority by a successful rebellion. It is very likely that Divākara Paṇḍita who henceforth played a dominant part in the Court as the High Priest had, in some way, contributed to his success. He performed the coronation ceremony of Jayavarman VI and his two successors.

Nothing is known of Jayavarman VI. He died in 1107 A.D. and was succeeded by his elder brother Dharaṇīndravarman I (No. 162). The latter being well advanced in age was unwilling to assume the burden of royalty, but had to yield to the wishes of the people, who were left without a protector at his brother's death. Dharaṇīndravarman was defeated by Sūryavarman II, the daughter's son of his sister (No. 180), and the latter ascended the throne in 1113 A.D. (No. 165). He is expressly said in two different Inss. (Nos. 165, 171) to have reunited the two kingdoms in Kambuja. It is obvious that one of these was ruled by Dharaṇīndravarman, and probably the other was under a descendant of Harṣavarman III, both of whom were defeated by Sūryavarman.[14] Sūryavarman was consecrated by Divākara Paṇḍita who also initiated him into the mysteries of Vrah Guhya (the Great Secret), probably a tantric cult. The king performed Koṭihoma, Lakṣahoma, and the Mahāhoma as well as various sacrifices to the ancestors (Nos. 167, 168). The cult of Bhadreśvara, whose sacred temple was in Vat Phu, the primitive capital of Kambuja, seems to have come into porminence about this time (No. 170). Sūryavarman further earned undying fame by constructing the famous Angkor Vat[14a] one of the wonders of the world. Sūryavarman sent two embassies to China in 1117 and 1121 A.D., thus resuming the diplomatic relations which were interrupted after the eighth century A.D. The Chinese Emperor conferred high titles on the Kambuja king whose dominions are said, in the Chinese annals, to have extended from Champā to Lower Burma and included the northern part of Malay Peninsula up to the Bay of Bandon. This is corro-

14. BEFEO. XXIX. p. 303.

14a. This has been conclusively proved by G. Coedès (*JA*. 11e serie Tome XV, 1920, pp. 96-100).

borated by other evidences.[15] Thus we see that in spite of internal troubles the limits of the Kambuja empire exceeded even those of the tenth century. The Kambuja king is said to have maintained 200,000 war elephants, and grandiloquent description is given of the royal tower.[16]

The Kambuja inscriptions refer in rapturous terms to the victories of Sūryavarman and his triumph over hostile kings, but they are very vague and do not give any specific information. He is said to have fought a terrible battle, in course of which he struck down his rival king from the head of his elephant and slew him (No. 171). This presumably refers to either Dharaṇīndravarman or the king of the line of Harṣavarman III who ruled over a part of Kambuja. We are further told that the kings of other islands whom he wanted to conquer voluntarily submitted to him and he himself marched into the countries of the enemies (No. 171). These probably refer to his military campaigns in N. Annam and Champā, the details of which are preserved in Annamese Annals and the inscriptions of Champā.

Sūryavarman sent one or more expeditions to Champā and reduced the northern part of it, the kingdom of Vijaya, almost to a vassal state of Kambuja. In 1128 he sent an expedition, 20,000 strong, against the kingdom of Annam, and invaded Nghe-an. At the same time he sent a fleet of 700 vessels, which with the support of the army of Champā was to attack Hatin. The army crossed the Annamite Hills by the pass of Ha-trai and descended to the valley of Pho-giang. There they halted and waited for the fleet and the Cham army. But these did not arrive in time, and in the meantime the Annamite troops fell upon the Kambuja army and defeated it. The Kambuja general was killed and his army beat retreat. The fleet and the Cham army arrived after a few months, and deprived of the support of the Kambuja army, retreated, after having ravaged the coast of Nghe-an and Tnan-hoa. In 1132 A.D. the army of Kambuja, with that of Champā, again invaded Nghe-an, but was easily repulsed by the

15. For the Chinese account cf. Ma-Twan-Lin's *Meridionaux* translated by Hervey de St. Denis, p. 485. The bas-reliefs of Angkor depict Siamese soldiers as fighting under Kambuja generals (*BEFEO*, XXV, p. 18; *IHQ*. I, p. 618; *BCAI*. 1911, p. 103).

16. These and other details are given in the Chinese account (see preceding footnote).

governor of Than-hoa. The two countries then made peace with Annam and sent an embassy in 1135. Two years later, the Kambuja army again invaded Nghe-an and was again easily repulsed. The Cham army did not join the Kambujas in this last expedition and observed the peace with Annam.[17] Probably to punish this desertion or taking advantage of the accession of a new king, Jaya Harivarman in the southern part of Champā, Sūryavarman decided to complete the subjugation of Champā. . A detailed account of the campaign is given in inscriptions of Champā, which may be summed up as follows.[18]

Scarcely had the king ascended the throne when the king of Kambuja commanded Śaṅkara, the foremost among his generals, to go and fight him in the plain of Rājapura. Śaṅkara was aided by a large number of troops from Vijaya i.e. the portion of Champā subject to Kambuja. Harivarman met the hostile army at Chak-lyan (probably the village of Chakling in the southern part of the valley of Phanrang, in the neighbourhood of the rock of Batau Tablah which contains an inscription describing the battle) and gained a great victory. As the Myson inscription tells us: "Jaya Harivarman fought against the general Śaṅkara and all the other Cambodian generals with their troops. They died in the field of battle." This happened in 1147 A.D. Next year "the king of Kambuja sent an army thousand times stronger than the previous one to fight in the plain of Vīrapura". Harivarman met them at the field of Kayev and completely defeated them.

Having defeated the two armies sent against him, Harivarman now felt powerful enough to take the offensive. The king of Kambuja did not underrate the danger. He hastily consecrated Harideva, the younger brother of his first queen, as king of Vijaya, and "commanded various generals to lead the Cambodian troops and protect prince Harideva until he became king in the city of Vijaya." Jaya Harivarman also marched towards that city and probably re-took it before the arrival of Harideva. In any case the two hostile armies met at the plain of Mahīsa "to the east of the temple of Guheśvara on the river Yami," and Harideva was defeated and killed. "Jaya Harivarman destroyed the king Harideva with all his Cham and Cambodian generals and the Cham and Cambodian troops; they all perished."

17. *BEFEO*, XVIII, No. 3, p. 33.
18. *Champa*, Part I pp. 96 ff; Part II, pp. 179-80, 193.

This battle took place in 1149 A.D.[18a] Next year the Kambuja king sent an expedition against Annam. The Kambuja army started in autumn, and the monsoon proved disastrous. The troops suffered heavily from fever during their passage over the Annamite hills and they were so weakened when they reached Nghe-an, that they retreated without any fight.[19]

Thus the foreign expeditions of Sūryavarman proved disastrous and it had serious repercussion on the fortunes of Kambuja. The history of this kingdom after the death of Sūryavarman II is obscure, but it is definitely known to have suffered much both from internal dissensions and the series of defeats inflicted by the king of Champā.

The last known date of Śūryavarman II is 1145 A.D. though he probably ruled for some years more. He had the posthumous title Paramaviṣṇuloka.[19a] He was probably succeeded by Dharaṇīndravarman II, the son of his maternal uncie, though we are not quite certain about it. Dharaṇīndravarman's queen was the daughter of king Harṣavarman, who is most probably to be identified with king Harṣavarman III.[20] We do not know anything about Dharaṇīndravarman II, not even whether he was the legitimate heir to the throne or got it by peaceful means. The same uncertainty prevails about the next king Yaśovarman II, though we know some details of his reign from an inscription of Jayavarman VII found at Bantay Chmar.[21] It tells us that Yaśovarman was faced with a rebellion headed by Bharata Rāhu Sambuddhi. Evidently the rebellion assumed at one time serious proportions,

18a. As the last known date of Sūryavarman II is 1145 A.D. a part of this campaing which ended in 1149 A.D., and the subsequent troubles created in Champā by the Kambuja king (*Champa*, pp. 97-8) might belong to the next reign or reigns.

19. *BEFEO*, XVIII, No. 3. p. 34.

19a. Cf *JA*. 11e Serie, Tome XV, 1920, pp. 96-100.

20. *BEFEO*, XXIX, p. 327.

21. King Yaśovarman mentioned in the Bsntay Chmar Ins. (No. 182) was identified by Aymonier (II. pp. 344-5) with Yaśovarman I and the revolution and campaign against Champā, mentioned in this record, were placed during his reign. This view was followed by all the writers on the subject until Coedès demonstrated that the events related in the record refer to a new king Yaśovarman II of the 12th century A.D. For the account that follows of the two hitherto unknown kings, Yaśovarman II and Tribhuvanādityavarmnan, and prince Śrīndra-Kumāra cf. Coedès' brilliant exposition in *BEFEO*, XXIX, pp. 305 ff.

for we are told that the rebels attacked even the palace itself and the royalist troops in the capital took to flight. Prince Śrīndrakumāra,[22] son of the future king Jayavarman VII, came to the rescue of the king. He himself fought in person with the rebels and defeated them.

It is in connection with this fight that we come across the term *Sanjak,* which presumably means a chief bound by a special oath or obligation to defend the person of the king or a prince. When Śrīndrakumāra came out to fight with the rebels, his body was covered by two *Sanjaks,* who were killed before his very eyes. The king showed appreciation of their service in a befitting manner. Posthumous honours were bestowed on them and their statues were installed in shrines. The fact that the inscriptions refer to these statues as gods shows that they were deified like kings. Needless to add that the king bestowed wealth, favours and honours on the members of their families.

The rebellion did not seriously affect the solidarity of the kingdom. For Yaśovarman felt powerful enough to send an expedition against the kingdom of Champā, led by the same prince Śrīndrakumāra. At first his enterprise proved successful. He seized the fort which Jaya Indravarman, king of Champā, had built on Mount Vek, and placed a Cham general on the throne of that kingdom. But the re–organised Cham troops caught Śrīndrakumāra in an ambush and surrounded him. He was forced to retreat, though continually fighting with his enemy, and took shelter on Mount Trayachur. The Cham troops besieged him on the mountain, but the prince fought his way down to the foot of the hill, and succeeded in breaking through the enemy line. On this occasion, too, he owed his life to the deliberate self-sacrifice of two of his *Sanjaks* who gave their lives in defending his person. As on the previous occasion, the king conferred posthumous honours on the two heroes and installed their statues in a shrine. Though the prince safely returned with his army to his kingdom the whole expedition was an ignominious failure.

The prince Śrīndrakumāra died while young, and his statue also was placed in the same shrine where those of his four faithful *Sanjaks* were installed.

22. *Sri* is a part of the name, and not an honorific prefix.

The war with Champā, however, continued, and another expedition was sent to Vijaya (central Champā), probably under the future king Jayavarman VII. About this time, and evidently taking advantage of the absence of royal troops in Champā, another rebellion took place in Kambuja, headed by Tribhuvanādityavarman. As soon as he heard of this outbreak, Jayavarman returned with his troops to Kambuja, but he was too late. For Yaśovarman II was defeated and killed and Tribhuvanādityavarman had ascended the throne of Kambuja. This took place before 1166 A.D. Jayavarman evidently could do nothing and simply bided his opportunity which was not long in coming.

The facts recorded above prove that Yaśovarman II was connected with the royal family, for otherwise it is difficult to account for the loyal services rendered to him both by Jayavarman and his son Śrīndrakumāra. Tribhuvanādityavarman, on the other hand, appears to be a usurper and adventurer, having no connection with the royal family, but merely an official (*bhṛtya*). This new king of Kambuja was involved in a prolonged fight with Champā, with disastrous consequences. Fortunately, this campaign is referred to not only in the inscriptions of Kambuja (Nos. 180, 181) but also in the Chinese annals,[23] and both represent Jaya Indravarman, king of Champā, as the victor. According to the Kambuja inscription Jaya Indravarman invaded Kambuja with a big army and Tribhuvanādityavarman was defeated and killed. But the Chinese account gives some details of the campaign. We are told that Jaya Indravarman invaded Kambuja in 1170 A.D. (or three years earlier)[24] and the war went on for seven years without any decisive result. At last the Cham king equipped a fleet and sent a naval expedition in 1177 A.D. The fleet sailed up the Mekong river and reached the capital city, and Jaya Indravarman plundered the capital and then retired, carrying an immense booty with him. According to the Kambuja inscription the Kambuja king, evidently Tribhuvanādityavarman, was killed in this fight,[25] but Kambuja

23. cf. *BEFEO*. II, p. 130 and Maspero—*Le Royaume de Champā* p. 164, where full references are given. The account is also given in *Champa*, pp. 103-4.

24. Maspero (*op. cit.*) gives the date on Chinese authority but the Po Nagar Ins. (in Champā) of Jaya Indravarman, dated 1167 A.D., refers to his expedition against Kambuja (*Champā*, Part II. p. 198).

25. This is also mentioned in one Chinese account (*BEFEO*. II, p. 130) though Maspero discredited it on grounds, which do not appear to be quite strong (*op. cit.* p. 164, f.n. 6).

was saved by the heroism of Jayavarman. He defeated the Chams in a naval engagement[26] and made himself master of the kingdom of Kambuja, four years later.

With the accession of Jayavarman VII in A.D. 1181 (No. 178) we are again on the firm ground. He was the last great king of Kambuja and we know a great deal about him, his military campaigns, his religious foundations and his works of public utility.

As regards the first, he attained conspicuous success in his wars with Champā, the eternal enemy of Kambuja. As already noted above, he had probably fought in Champā on behalf of Yaśovarman II. The war was renewed after he had ascended the throne. According to the Ins. No. 177 (v. 28) he took the Cham king prisoner and then released him. According to the Chinese account of Ma Twan Lin, Jayavarman fully avenged the sack of the Kambuja capital by the king of Champā. The King of Kambuja, we are told, invaded Champā, dethroned its prince, and put one of his own men in his place, and for long Champā remained a vassal state of Kambuja.[27]

Fortunately the Inss. of Champā supply us very interesting and detailed information about the war between Champā and Kambuja[28] which was begun in 1190 A.D. by the aggressive campaign of Jaya Indravarman on Vatuv king of Champā. The Kambuja king Jayavarman VII sent an expedition to check his advance and invade Champā.

The leader of this expedition, who was ultimately destined to play an important part in history, was Śrī Sūryavarmadeva, prince Śrī Vidyānandana. He was apparently an inhabitant of Champā, but betook himself early in life to Kambuja (1182 A.D.). The king of Kambuja welcomed him and employed his services on occasions. Thus we read: "During his stay at Kambuja, a dependent town of Kambuja called Malyan, inhabited by a multitude of bad men, revolted ageinst the king of Kambuja. The latter, seeing

26. The scenes of this naval victory are perhaps depicted in the sculptures of Bayon and Bantay Chmar (*BEFEO.* XXIX, p. 326).

27. Cf. also *BEFEO.* II. 130 for other Chinese references to this. The date of his expedition, as given in the Chinese accounts, is not correct (Maspero-*op. cit.* p. 164. f.n. 8).

28 Cf. *Champa*, pp. 106 ff. from which the following account is quoted. The passages within quotation marks are extracts from Cham Inscriptions,

the prince well-versed in arms, ordered him to lead the Kambuja troops and take the town of Malyan. He did all that the king of Kambuja desired."

The king of Kambuja, pleased at his valour, conferred on him the dignity of Yuvarāja, and when war broke out with Champā, as related above, he "sent the prince at the head of Kambuja troops in order to take Vijaya, and defeat the king Jaya Indravarman On Vatuv. Śrī Sūryavarmadeva obtained a complete victory. He captured the king of Champā and had him conducted to Kambuja by the Kambuja troops."

The king of Kambuja now divided Champā into two portions. He placed his own brother-in-law, Sūrya Jayavarmadeva prince In, as king of the northern part with Vijaya as capital, while Sūryavarmadeva, prince Śrī Vidyānandana, the victorious general, became king of the southern portion with his capital at Rājapura in Panraṅ.

Sūryavarmadeva prince Śrī Vidyānandana defeated a number of 'thieves or pirates', apparently the adherents of the late regime that had revolted against him, and reigned in peace at Rājapura. The northern kingdom, however, was soon lost to Kambuja. Within two years, prince Raṣupati, apparently a local chief, led a revolt against the Kambuja usurper, Śrī Sūrya Jayavarmadeva prince In. The latter was defeated, and returned to Kambuja, while Raṣupati ascended the throne under the name of Śrī Jaya Indravarmadeva.

The king of Kambuja now sent an expedition against Vijaya (1192 A.D.). With a view, probably, to conciliate the national sentiments by placing the captured king of Champā Śrī Jaya Indravarman Oṅ Vatuv on the throne, as a dependent of Kambuja, he sent him along with this expedition. The Kambuja troops first went to Rājapura. There the king Sūryavarmadeva prince Śrī Vidyānandana put himself at their head, and marched against Vijaya. He captured Vijaya and defeated and killed Jaya Indravarman (Raṣupati).

The victorious king of Rājapura now ascended the throne of Vijaya and the whole of Champā was again re-united under him. Jaya Indravarman On Vatuv, the king of Champā, being deprived of the throne, fled to Amarāvatī. There he collected a large number of troops and advanced against Vijaya. "The king defeated him, compelled him to fall back on Traik, and there captured him and put him to death." Henceforth Sūryavarmadeva Vidyānandana ruled over the whole of Champā without opposition (1192 A.D.).

But he had shortly to reckon with the king of Kambuja whom he had so basely betrayed. In 1193 an expedition was sent against him, but he gained an easy victory. Next year the expedition was repeated on a larger scale.

"In Śaka 1116 (1194 A.D.) the king of Kambuja sent a large number of generals with all sorts of arms. They came to fight with the prince. The latter fought at Jai Ramya-Vijaya, and vanquished the generals of the Kambuja army."

But the king was not destined to enjoy his sovereignty for a long time. He was defeated in 1203 A.D. by his paternal uncle, called Yuvarāja (or son of Yuvarāja) Mnagahṅa Oṅ Dhanapati or Yuvarāja Oṅ Dhanapatigrāma, who was sent by the king of Kambuja against him.

The career of this Yuvarāja was analogous in many respects to that of king Sūryavarman himself. He, too, lived as an exile in the Court of Kambuja and obtained the favours of the king by successfully suppressing the revolt of Malyan. It is just possible that these two Cham chiefs, uncle and nephew, both went together to Kambuja and the Malyan revolt, which both claim to have subdued, was the self-same military expedition in which both of them took part. But the nephew soon surpassed the uncle and, as we have seen above, ultimately became the king of Champā.

The king of Kambuja, twice baffled in his attempt to defeat him, at last sent the uncle against the nephew. In 1203 A.D. king Sūryavarman was defeated and the Yuvarāja On Dhanapati ruled over Champā.

The Yuvarāja Dhanapatigrāma, who now ruled over Champā, had a hard time before him. Rebellion broke out in various parts of the kingdom. The most formidable was one led by Putau Ājñā Ku, but it was put down by the Yuvarāja. "Then Putau Ājñā Ku revolted. He conquered from Amarāvatī as far as Pidhyaṅ. The king of Kambuja commanded the Yuvarāja to lead the troops of Kambuja and capture Putau Ājñā Ku. He captured him and sent him to Kambuja according to the desire of the king".

The king of Kambuja, pleased at his valour, conferred high dignities on him, and apparently formally appointed him as the ruler of Champā in 1207 A.D.

It appears, however, that Champā was at this time very hard pressed by the Annamites. The Cho Dinh Inscription tells us: "Then (sometime after 1207 A.D.) the Siamese and the Pukam (people of Pugan in Lower Burma) came from Kambuja and a battle took place with the Annamites. The Kambuja generals led the troops which opposed the Annamites and the loss on both sides was very great." The Annamite documents inform us that the Chams aided by the Cambodians attacked Nghe-An in 1216 and 1218, but the governor of the Province dispersed them. It would thus appear that since about 1207 A.D. a series of battles followed, in which victory more often inclined to the Annamites.

These long-drawn battles must have exhausted the Kambujas. As a matter of fact, the series of warfares in which they were involved ever since 1190 A.D. when they conquered Champā, must have proved too great a burden for the people and, to make matters worse, the Thais in Siam at this time began to press them hard from the west. At last in 1220 A.D. the Kambujas evacuated Champā, and a formal peace was probably concluded with Aṅśa-rāja of Turai Vijaya in 1222 A.D.

It is not definitely known whether Jayavarman VII was still alive when this final withdrawal took place. Most probably he had ceased to rule some time before it, for we do not know, even approximately, the year of his death.[29]

But the credit of conquering Champā and making it a vassal state of Kambuja belongs to him. It was the crowning triumph at the end of an age-long struggle which extended the frontier of the Kambuja empire to the China Sea on the east. But Jayavarman VII did not confine his military activities to the eastern frontier of his kingdom. On the western side, too, he appears to have attained some success against the kingdom of Pagan. Since the middle of the eleventh century A.D. this kingdom grew very powerful and subjugated Ramaṇṇadeśa, thereby extending its authority over the whole of central and southern Burma. According to the Chinese chronicles[30] Pagan was annexed to Kambuja towards the close of the twelfth century A.D. Whether the Chinese mean the whole of Pagan or some part of it adjacent to Kambuja empire, such as

29. The view, generally accepted, that Jayavarman VII died in 1201 A.D., has been proved to be wrong by Coedès (*BEFEQ*. XXV. pp. 393-4; XXIX, p. 328).

30. Aymonier, III, 528.

Pegu, we cannot say. But in any case it shows a further expansion of the Kambuja empire beyond its western limits in the tenth and eleventh century A.D. The credit of this conquest certainly belongs to Jayavarman VII, though unfortunately we have no details in his inscriptions beyond a vague reference that he defeated a king (No. 179). It must be remembered, however, that the Cham inscriptions, noted above, refer to the people of Pukan (Pagan) as having served in the Kambuja army. Ins. No. 177 also says that the men of Champā and Pukan were employed as servants in the temples. No doubt they were mostly prisoners from Burma and Champā The Ceylonese chronicle Mahāvaṁsa has preserved a story to the effect that a princess sent by king Parākramabāhu of Ceylon (1164-1197 A.D.) to Kambuja was seized by the Burmese king who also imprisoned the Ceylonese envoys on the ground that they were sent to Kambuja.[30a] This seems to be an echo of the hostility between the kings of Kambuja and Pagan.

Jayavarman VII thus ruled over an empire which stretched from the Bay of Bengal to the Sea of China. The central regions in the Indo-Chinese Peninsula and the northern part of Malay Peninsula formed part of his empire as in the tenth century A.D.

The religious foundations and works of public utility undertaken by Jayavarman VII were on a scale befitting the mighty empire over which he ruled. The account of royal donations contained in the Ta Prohm Ins. (No. 177) makes interesting reading and reveals the magnitude of the resources and depth of religious sentiments of the king It concerns the Rājavihāra i.e., the temple of Ta Prohm and its adjuncts where the king set up an image of his mother as Prajñā-pāramitā. It is not possible here to record all the details but a few facts may be noted. Altogether 66,625 persons were employed in the service of the deities of the temple and 3,400 villages were given for defraying its expenses. There were 439 Professors and 970 scholars studying under them, making a total of 1409, whose food and other daily necessaries of life were supplied. There were altogether 566 groups of stone houses and 288 groups of brick. Needless to say that the other articles, of which a minute list is given, were in the same proportion, and they included huge quantities of gold and silver, 35 diamonds, 40,620 pearls and 4,540 other precious stones. All these relate to a

30a. *Mahāvaṁsa*, ch. 76, vv. 21-35. *JASB.* XII, pp. 197-201; *BEFEO.* II, p. 130.

single group of temples. And the inscription informs us that there were 798 temples and 102 hospitals in the whole kingdom, and these are given every year 117,200 *khārikās* of rice, each *khārikā* being equivalent to 3 maunds 8 seers. In conclusion the king expresses the hope that by his pious donations, his mother might be delivered from the ocean of births (*bhavāvdhi*).

Of the 102 hospitals mentioned above, the site of 15 can be determined by means of inscriptions which record their foundations.[31] These inscriptions are almost identical and lay down detailed regulations about the hospitals. They give us a very good idea of the system of medical treatment organised by the state,[32] but require separate treatment and cannot be discussed here.

Jayavarman VII also established 121 *Vahnigṛha* or *dharamsālās* along the principal routes within his kingdom for the convenience of pilgrims and other travellers.[33]

Jayavarman VII was a devout Buddhist and received the posthumous name Mahā-parama-saugata. Many of his records express in beautiful language the typically Buddhist view of life, particularly the feelings of charity and compassion towards the whole universe.

Jayavarman VII reigned for more than twenty years. His death which nearly coincides with the closing of the twelfth century A.D. constitutes an important landmark in the history of Kambuja. For it is now generally recognised that the eleventh and twelfth centuries A.D. form the most glorious period in the annals of the great Hindu colony. It saw the greatest expansion of the Kambuja empire which extended from Lower Burma to Annam, and reached the Bay of Bengal on the west and the China Sea on the East. In the north, most of the Thai principalities in Laos acknowledged its suzerainty and its boundaries touched those of the Chinese Empire. In the south it not only comprised the whole of Siam. Cambodia and Cochin-China, but also a part of Malay Peninsula. The wild peoples of the comparatively inaccessible uplands of Laos were brought under the civilising influence of

31. *BEFEO*, XL, p. 344.
32. *BEFEO*, III, p. 18.
33. *BEFEO*, XL. p. 347.

the Hinduised Khmers, and the onward march of Hindu culture followed in the wake of the victorious campaigns of the Kambuja kings. The glory of the Hindu culture is seen at its best in these palmy days of the Kambuja Empire. The cultivation of Sanskrit literature, both secular and religious, reached the highest development in Kambuja during this period, and the themes of the two great Indian epics adorned the walls of its most famous monuments. High priests, learned in Hindu and Buddhist canons, obtained a dominant position in state and society, and we possess elaborate and lengthy records of quite a large number of eminent Brahman families. They typified the essence of Indian culture and were mainly instrumental in transplanting and diffusing the higher intellectual, moral and spiritual life of India on the soil of Kambuja. The long and elaborate *praśastis* of the Kambuja kings, though poor in respect of data for political history, are rich in supplying materials for the reconstruction of the spiritual life of the people. The kings and grandees of Kambuja, not to speak of its priests and *ācāryas* housed in the hundreds of *āśramas* reared by the piety of the rulers and nobles, were imbued with the impulses of that higher life in man which forms such a distinct characteristic of Indian civilisation. It is not merely the externals of Hindu civilisation but the very essence of the Hindu view of life that is unfolded before our eyes as we study the records of this period, and review the achievements of the greatest kings of Kambuja. What, for example, can be a nobler sentiment than that which inspired king Jayavarman VII in founding the hospitals, more than 100 in number, all over his kingdom? In the record of the foundations we read:

> "*Dehinām deha-rogo yan-manorogo rujattarām* |
> *Rāṣṭra-duḥkham hi bhartṛṇām duḥkhan=duḥkhan=tu nātmanaḥ* ||

"The bodily pain of the diseased became in him (king Jayavarman VII) a mental agony more tormenting than the former. For the real pain of a king is the pain of his subjects, not that of his own (body)."

This noble sentiment, which combines the idealism of the Kauṭilyan king with the piety and humanity of Asoka, was not a mere pious wish or thought but was actually translated into action by the elaborate system of remedial measures with a network of 102 hospitals as its nucleus.

The eleventh and twelfth centuries A.D. also produced the most notable monuments in Kambuja which still excite the wonder and admiration of the world. It has not been possible for me to review the history of art in Kambuja in course of these lectures, because its evolution and chronology is still a matter of dispute and the subject therefore requires a separate and detailed treatment in a series of lectures wholly devoted to it. But viewed as a whole, the monuments of Kambuja, both by their massive character and unparalleled grandeur, form the most brilliant testimony to the richness and splendour of a civilisation of which the written records give but an imperfect picture. It would be no exaggeration to say that in respect of architecture the Indian colony of Kambuja far surpasses the mother-land, even though the achievements of the latter are by no means of mean order. In spite of uncertainties of chronology we may refer a few monuments, with tolerable certainty, to this period which constitutes in so many ways the most memorable one in the history of Kambuja.

The most famous of the monuments of Kambuja, *viz.*, Angkor Vat was built by king Sūryavarman II who ruled between 1113 and 1145 A.D. The Baphuon, another noble monument, was formerly referred to the 9th and 10th centuries A.D. but is now regarded as belonging to the reign of Udayādityavarman II (1049–1066 A.D.).[34] The famous Angkor Thom, with its gate-towers, ramparts and ditches, and the Temple of Bayon in the centre of the city, were formerly attributed to Yaśovarman I (889–908 A.D.) but are now believed by some to be the work of Jayavarman VII,[35] who ascended the throne in the year 1181 A.D. Another famous monument, that of Bantay Chmar, whch was formerly attributed to Jayavarman II (9th century) is also referred by some to Jayavarman VII[36] and others to Yaśovarman II[37] (1160-1180 A.D.). In short, whereas the majority of the splendid monuments of Kambuja were formerly placed in the 9th and 10th centuries A.D., their date is now brought down by nearly two or three hundred years, and instead of Jayavarman II and Yaśovarman I, the four successive kings Sūryavarman II, Dharaṇīndravarman II, Yaśovarman II and Jayavarman VII, whose reigns practically cover the

34. *BEFEO*, XXXI, p. 18.
35. *BEFEO*. XXVIII, p. 81.
36. *Ibid*, p. 100.
37. *BEFEO*. XXXV, p. 181.

whole of the twelfth century A.D., appear to be the great builders of Kambuja monuments. We must, therefore, give up the old idea that the twelfth century was a period of decay in the history of Kambuja, and rather regard it as the period of the greatest glory of Kambuja.

It is not possible in the present course of lectures to give such a detailed description, even of the most famous monuments of Kambuja, as would convey a fair idea of their nature and artistic excellence. I would therefore merely attempt to indicate, in a general way, the special features which characterise them.

The earliest series of monuments at Angkor consist of isolated temples which show great resemblance with Indian temples. But gradually a new style is evolved in the eleventh and twelfth centuries A.D., first by the introduction of gallery, and later still, by pyramidal construction in several stages. The combination of these two features results in a series of concentric galleries, enclosing each successive stage of the pyramid, with a crowning tower at the centre of the top or the highest stage. Similar towers are added at the four corners of each stage of the pyramid, and finally we have the *gopurams* at one or all the four faces, each consisting of a gateway with a vestibule, surmounted by an ornamental tower in the form of a stepped pyramid as we see in South India. The central and corner towers are of the North-Indian or Śikhara style. An innovation is introduced in Bayon, where the towers are capped by four heads facing the four directions. The wide ditches surrounding the temples and cities, with paved causeways over them, form an important feature of construction, and the figures of a series of giants pulling the body of a serpent, which form the balustrades of the causeway on its two sides, are justly regarded as one of the most ingenious and interesting architectural devices to be seen anywhere in the world. The gallery, referred to above, is in its final shape, a long narrow running chamber with vaulted roof, supported by a wall on one side and a series of pillars on the other. It has a *veranda* with a half-vaulted roof of lower height supported by columns of smaller dimensions. The walls of these galleries are generally covered with continuous friezes of bas-reliefs and other sculptures.

An idea of the massive character of these monuments may be had from the measurements of Angkor Vat. The moat or ditch surrounding the temple and running close to its boundary walls is more than 650 ft. wide. This is spanned by a broad stone causeway leading to the wall of enclosure which completely surrounds the temple and has a total length of two miles and a half. The broad paved avenue which runs from the western gateway to the first gallery is 520 yds. long and raised 7 ft. above the ground. The first gallery measures 265 yds. east to west and 224 from north to south, with a total running length of nearly 1000 yds. The central tower, on the third or highest gallery, rises to a height of more than 210 ft.

About a mile to the north of Angkor Vat lie the ruins of Angkor Thom, the capital city of Jayavarman VII, formerly believed to be that of Yaśovarman I. The town was surrounded by a high wall made of limonite with a ditch beyond it, 110 yds. wide. The ditch has a total length of nearly 8½ miles and its sides are paved with enormous blocks of stone. The enclosing walls were pierced by huge gates which gave access to the city by means of five grand avenues each 33 yds. wide and running straight from one end to the other. Each gateway consisted of a huge arched opening more than 30 ft. high and 15 ft. wide, and surmounted by four huge heads placed back to back. The town was square in shape, each side measuring about two miles. The grand avenues converge to the Temple of Bayon which occupies almost the central position of the city and is justly regarded as the masterpiece of Kambuja architecture. To the north of the Bayon is a great public square, a sort of forum, about 765 yds. long and 165 yds. wide, surrounded by famous structures such as the Baphuon, the Phimeanakas, the Terrace of Honour etc. The Bayon is the largest temple in Angkor Thom, and though constructed on the same principle as Angkor Vat, the arrangements of the galleries are more complex. Its lowest gallery is about 165 yds. long from east to west and 109 yds. from north to south. The central conical tower is crowned by four heads, probably of Brahmā, and its summit is about 150 ft. high from the ground level. Bayon contains some of the finest sculptures to be seen in Kambuja.

These few details would serve to convey an idea of the massive character of Kambuja temples. But it is not by their massive form alone that they appeal to us. Their fine proportions, the general symmetry of the plan, and above all the decorative sculptures invest them with a peculiar grandeur.

The sculptures in Kambuja, both bas-reliefs and figures in the round, also attained to a high level of excellence. Here, again, we find that while the earlier sculptures show a close affinity with

Indian models, specially Gupta art, new elements are added in course of time which give a distinctive character to Kambuja sculpture. The peculiar smiling countenance, with half-closed eyes, of divine figures, known as the smile of Angkor, has been variously interpreted, and opinions differ on its aesthetic values. It has been suggested that this unchanging and elusive smile which mysteriously reflects the illumination of inward *nirvāṇa* and expresses supreme Buddhist beatitude is the most notable contribution of Khmer art. But this smile of Angkor is not confined to Buddhist heads alone, as is generally supposed. It appears in Brahmanical images and should, therefore, be regarded as a divine expression rather than anything peculiarly Buddhist. Although the figures often show traces of Khmer physiognomy, some of the best figures, exhibiting plastic quality of a high order, are marked by the purity of Aryan profile.

The bas-reliefs which adorn the temples of Kambuja form the most important class of Kambuja sculpture. The earlier specimens show the figures in fairly high relief like those of Java and India, but gradually the depth of the relief is decreased till the figures are merely incised or scratched on the surface and the whole thing looks like a tapestry on stone. But subject to this limitation the bas-relief sculptures show balance, harmony and rhythm of a high order. They are marked for their narrative skill and cover a wide range of fields embracing almost all phases of human and animal lives. The scenes are full of life and movements and are graceful without being exuberant. The vast lengths of galleries covered by these interminable scenes display the decorative faculties of Kambuja art at their very best, but these are duly subordinated to the architecture.

It is needless to pursue this topic any further. But whether we look at the massive temples with elegant proportions or the sculptures which adorn their walls, we cannot but pay the greatest tribute to their truly classic composition of the highest order.

If art is an expression of national character and a fair index of the culture and civilisation of a people, Kambuja easily takes the leading position among the Indian colonies in Indo-China and constitutes an immortal landmark and the greatest living testimony to the splendour of the civilisation of which it is a product. Until recently no one doubted the Indian origin of this art, but lately a school of critics has sought to establish that this developed phase of Kambuja architecture and sculpture is of purely Khmer origin and is not indebted to India in any way. They concede the purely Indian origin of the earlier structures but hold that the noble monuments of the 11th and 12th century do not owe anything to Indian influence or inspiration, but were original inventions of the local artists. This is not the place to enter into a detailed discussion of this question, but according to a more rational view the Kambuja architecture followed a regular course of development from the purely Indian type with which it started. It underwent a process of evolution such as we notice even in different parts of India itself, in different ages, and while the local genius and environments added new conceptions of beauty and principles of construction, it is as unreasonable to ignore Indian influence upon the monuments of Kambuja as to dissociate the culture and civilisation of Kambuja in other spheres from those of India. If we study for example the palaeography and iconography we find the same phenomena. The earlier alphabets and images are hardly distinguishable from those of India, but gradually both undergo slow and steady transformation. The fully developed Kambuja script of the twelfth century A.D. shows an altogether different aspect, and it would be difficult to regard it as Indian unless one studies the process of evolution. Similarly we find new iconographic features, new names of divinities, and even new conceptions of religion, not met with in India. The same has been the case also with art and architecture. And this is only what we could expect in a living society. It is to be noted that the Indian colonisation in the Far East was not an imperialism in any form, political or economic. It transfused new blood, in the shape of the cultural heritage of India, to create new life and spirit on alien soils. It transformed the weaker and the more backward by fresh vitality, and so long as this life-giving force was there the people were quickened by new impulses and did not merely imitate but developed healthy lives of their own on the foundations well and truly laid by the Indians. What the Indian element meant in their life and civilisation is best seen when this perennial fountain-source ceased to flow. In proportion to the lack of fresh vitalising forces from India the culture and civilisation of Kambuja showed signs of decline, and then came the inevitable end. It is not perhaps a mere coincidence that the two Indian colonies of Champā and Kambuja were overwhelmed by two branches of the Thais in the 13th century A.D. when India herself lay prostrate under the foreign invaders. The same phenomena are also noticed in Java. This sudden collapse of the culture and civilisation in these Indian colonies at the very moment when India herself lost her independence and was submerged in darkness constitutes the most important testimony to the influence she exercised over their growth and development.

EPILOGUE

We do not propose to trace the history of Kambuja beyond the twelfth century A.D. but would merely complete this sketch by a very brief outline of the subsequent events.

Jayavarman VII was succeeded by Indravarman II. The latter died in 1243 A.D. (No. 186).

The next king known to us is Jayavarman VIII who abdicated the throne in 1295–96 A.D. and received the posthumous name Parameśvara. It is difficult to say whether he was the immediate successor of Indravarman. In that case he would have reigned for 52 years.[37a] This is not unlikely, for we know that he ruled up to ripe old age. For it is said in the Bantay Srei Ins. of his son-in-law and successor that the earth, suffering from the troubles of the reign of an old man, was now freed from them by the vigilance of a young king.[38] But nevertheless Kambuja was powerful enough to refuse the payment of tribute asked for by the Mongol Emperors of China.[39]

The abdication of Jayavarman VIII was followed by a struggle for succession. The old king designated his son-in-law Śrīndravarman to be his successor, but his son made an attempt to seize the throne. Śrīndravarman mutilated and imprisoned his brother-in–law and ascended the throne in 1296.[40]

Whether the young king was able to remove "the thorns and brambles which had grown up" during the preceding reign—to use his own expression—it is difficult to say. During his reign a Chinese embassy came to Angkor Thom (1296 A.D.) and Cheu

37a. In describing the succession of kings after Jayavarman VII I have followed Finot's interpretation of the Ins. No. 186. It appears to me, however, that there was possibly a king named Śrī Śrīndrajayavarman after Jayavarman VIII, who was succeeded by his son-in-law Indravarman in 1295 or 1296 A.D. There would thus be two reigns between 1243 and 1296 A.D.

38. *BEFEO*. XXXV, p. 395.

39. *BEFEO*. II, p. 131.

40. This is reported by Cheu Ta-kuan; *cf.* also Ins. No. 185, v. 41.

Ta-kuan who accompanied it wrote the famous account of the manners and customs of Kambuja.[41]

Śrīndravarman abdicated the throne and was succeeded in 1308 (No. 185) by Yuvarāja Śrīndrajayavarman who was related to him (No. 186 vv. 47-8).

Only another king Jayavarma-Parameśvara is known from the Kambuja inscriptions (No. 187). Probably he was the successor of Śrīndrajayavarman and ascended the throne in 1327 A.D.[42] He is the last king known from inscriptions. The subsequent history of Kambuja can only be gathered from the Khmer chronicles which were composed at a considerably late period and cannot be regarded as trustworthy.

It will thus be seen that our knowledge of the history of Kambuja after the death of Jayavarman VII is very poor, and we hardly know anything reliable from the fourteenth century onwards.

But we can trace the general course of events which led to the decline and downfall of the Kambuja Empire. It appears that the Thais in the northern and western parts of the empire were organised under able military leaders and openly broke into revolt in Siam early in the thirteenth century A.D. A Thai chief Indrāditya founded an independent kingdom with Sukhodaya as capital some time about the middle of the thirteenth century A.D. After the conquest of the Thai principality of Yunnan by the great Mongol chief Kublai Khan in 1254, the newly founded Thai kingdom of Sukhodaya received a tremendous wave of Thai immigrants who fled from Yunnan. Ram Kahmheng, the famous Thai king of Sukhodaya towards the close of the 13th century, was a great conqueror. He carried his arms to Lower Burma on the west and to the heart of Kambuja on the east. Cheu Ta-kuan, who visited Kambuja shortly after, mentions that in the recent wars with the Siamese the region round Angkor was utterly devastated. But it is clear from the Chinese memoir that Kambuja was still a mighty kingdom and that Ram Kahmheng's invasion was more of the nature of a predatory raid than a regular conquest. The

41. The account has been translated by Remusat in *Nouveaux Melanges Asiatiques* (1829) pp. 77 ff, and by Pelliot in *BEFEO.* II, pp. 123-177 (for some corrections cf. *BEFEO.* XVIII (4) No. 9.).

42. *BEFEO.* XXVIII, pp. 145-6.

Thai kingdom of Sukhodaya came to an end soon after, and a new Thai dynasty which founded the kingdom of Ayuthia about 1350 A.D. soon made itself the master of the whole of Siam and Laos. To the east of Kambuja the Annamites gradually conquered nearly the whole of the kingdom of Champā by the fifteenth century. Kambuja was now hard pressed by these two important Thai powers on two sides who steadily encroached upon its territory. This simultaneous pressure from the two flanks proved the ruin of Kambuja. Its weak and helpless rulers tried to save themselves by playing off their two powerful enemies one against the other, but with disastrous consequences to themselves. For centuries Kambuja remained the victim of her two pitiless aggressive neighbours. At last shorn of power and prestige, and reduced to a petty state, Ang Duong, the king of Kambuja, in A.D. 1854, threw himself under the protection of the French, and thus the once mighty kingdom of Kambuja became, as it still is, a petty French Protectorate.

LIST OF INSCRIPTIONS (ARRANGED CHRONOLOGICALLY)

The following special abbreviations have been used:—

A=E. Aymonier-*Le Cambodge*, 3 Vols. (Paris, 1900-1903).

B=*Bulletin de l'Ecole Française d'Extrême-Orient.*

C=*Inscriptions du Cambodge* by G. Coedès (Hanoi, 1937).

Co=*Inscriptions Sanscrites du Cambodge* by M. Barth and A. Bergaigne (Paris 1885).

D=Dated.

Dt=District.

Dv=Division.

K, followed by a numerical figure, denotes the serial number of the inscription in the '*Listes générales des inscriptions et des Monuments* compiled by G. Coedés and H. Parmentier (Hanoi 1923) and in the '*Supplement*' published as Appendix to 'C'

L=L. de Lajonquière—*Inventaire descriptif des monuments du Cambodge,* 3 Vols. Paris 1902-11.

Loc=Locality.

Pr=Province.

'Ed.' denotes that the inscription has been properly edited, and 'R.' indicates that it is merely referred to, sometimes with a short summary, in the Journal or the Book named after them.
All the dates are in Śaka Era.

No. 1. Prasat Ak Yom Door Pillar Ins. D. 531.
R.B. XXXIII, p. 530, K. 749. Dt. Puok.
The most ancient Ins. employing Arabic Numerals—Foundation of the temple (dedicated to Gambhīreśvara) by Mratāṅ Kīrtigana —The temple is interred in Baray (western).

No. 2. Ankor Borei Stone Ins. D. 533.
R.B. XXXV, p. 491. K. 600. Dt. Prei Krabas.
It was found in the ruins of the village where once stood a fortified town which was formerly identified with Vyādhapura.

No. 3. Vat Vihar Tran Pillar Ins. D. 535.
R.B. XXXV, pp. 36, 142. K. 748, Pr. Kondal Stun.
The temple contains a *liṅga* and an image of Śiva with Pārvatī seated on his knee (p. 122, pl. XVII.A)

No. 4. Bayan temple Stele Ins. D. 546.
Ed. Co. No. V, p. 31. K. 13. Dt. Treang

No. 5. Phnom Bantay Nan Ins. of Bhavavarman (I or II)
Ed. Co. No. III, p. 26. R.A. II. 306. K. 213. Dt. Battambang.
Installation of a *liṅga* by the king.

No. 6. Prah Vihar Stele Ins. of Bhavavarman (I or II)
Ed. C. 3. K. 733, Dt. Kompon Len.
Endowment by poet Vidyāpuṣpa, master of the Pāśupata sect, and versed in various śāstras, *viz.* grammar, Vaiśeṣika and logic.

No. 7. Ponhear Hor Pillar Ins. of Bhavavarman (I or II)
Ed. Co. No. II, p. 21, K. 21. Dt. Tran.
Installation of Linga, Durgā, Śambhu-Viṣṇu, Visnu Trailokya-sāra.

No. 8. Han Chey Stele Ins. of Bhavavarman (I or II).
Ed. Co. No. 1, p. 8, K. 81.
Eulogy of the king and donations of a liṅga by an official.

No. 9. Veal Kantel Ins.. of Bhavavarman I.
Ed. Co. No. IV, p. 28, R.A. II, 180, K. 359.
Installation of an image of Tribhuvaneśvara by Brāhman Soma-śarman, husband of the daughter of Vīravarman, who was sister of Bhavavarman and mother of Hiraṇyavarman. Donation of complete texts of Mahābhārata, Rāmāyaṇa and Purāṇa.

No. 10. Thma Kre Ins. of Citrasena.
Ed. B. III, p. 212, K. 122.
Loc. on the Mekong south of Sambor.
One verse only—Installation of a Śiva-liṅga by Citrasena at the command (or with the approval) of his parent (*Mātā-pitror= anujñayā*). There are 2 replicas of this inscription (1) Cruoy Amphil. R.B. IV, p. 739. K. 116 (2) Tham Pet Thong (Rajaxima of Siam). R.B. XXII, p. 92, K. 514.

No. 11. Chan Nakhon (Phu Lokhon) Ins. of Mahendravarman
Ed. B. III. 442. R.L. II. 73. K. 363, Dt. Bassak.
Replicas (1-2) Khan Thevada. At the confluence of the Mun and the Mekong rivers.

(3) Tham Prasat

(4) Vat Xumphon at Muang Surin
B. XXII, pp. 57-59.

(5) Keng Tana (on the Mun)
B. XXII, p. 385.

For complete text cf. B. XXII, p. 58.
Installation of a liṅga on the top of the hill (or bull), as a sign of victory by Citrasena (grandson of Sārvabhauma, son of Vīravarman, youngest brother of Bhavavarman) who took the coronation name of Mahendravarman

No. 12. Prasat Pram Loven Stele Ins. of Īśānavarman.
R.A.I, p. 140. L. III, p. 478, K. 7. Dt. Sadec.
Installation of a divine image by the king.

No. 13. Sambor Prei Kuk Ins. of Īśānavarman.
R.B. XIII (1), p. 27, Dt. Kompon Svay.
Records a pious foundation by the queen Sākāra-mañjarī (*BCAJ*, 1912, p. 188).

No. 14. Sambor Prei Kuk Ins. of Īśānavarman.
R.B. XIII (1), p. 28.
Installation of an image of Prahanteśvara by the king.

No. 15. Sambor Prei Kuk Ins. of Īśānavarman.
R.B. XIII (1), p. 28; BCAI. 1912, p. 187.
Installation of the images of Sarasvatī, Nṛtteśvara and Nandin, and donations by the queen.

No. 16. Sambor Prei Kuk Ins. of Īśānavarman.
R.B. XIII (1), p. 28; *BCAI*, 1912, p. 188, Dt. Kampon Svay.
Mentions Īśānavarman and his relation with India, cf. the expression '*dakṣinā-patha-janmā*'.

No. 17. Sambor Prei Kuk Ins.
R.B. XIII (1), p. 28, Dt. Kampon Svay
Mentions Mahendravarman and Īśānavarman.

No. 18. Ang Pu (Vat Pu) Stele Ins. of Īśānavarman.
Ed Co. No. VIII, p. 47. K. 22, Dt. Tran.
Installation of an image and a *liṅga* of Śiva-Viṣṇu by Muni Īśānadatta.

No. 19. Sval Chno Stele Ins. of Īśānavarman.
Ed. Co. No. VII, p. 44. K. 80. Dt. Kandal.
Foundation of an *āśrama* by Ārya Vidyādeva.

No. 19A. Vat Sabab Ins. of Īśānavarman.
Ed. B. XXIV, p. 353. Loc. South-east of Chantabun.

No. 20. Sambor Prei Kuk. Pillar Ins. of Īśānavarman D. 549.
Ed. B. XXVIII, p. 44. K. 604. Dt. Kampon Svay.
Homage to Śrī Kadambeśvara—Eulogy of king Śrī Īśānavarman —one of his servants versed in Grammar, Vaiśeṣika, Nyāya Samīkṣa and Buddhism—erection of a *liṅga*—priest, a Pāśupata Brāhmaṇa—king referred to as lord of Tatandarapura (?).

No. 21. Prah vihar Kuk (or Vat Chakret) Stele Ins. cf Īśānavarman D. 549.
Ed. Co. No. VI, p. 38.
R.A.I., 237; L.I., 58; K. 60; Dt. Prei Ven (Ba Phnom).
Refers to king Īśānavarman and records erection of an image of Śiva-Viṣṇu by the vassal ruler of Tāmrapura.

No. 22. Vat Kdei Aṅ (Ang Chumnik) Stele Ins. D. 550.
Ed. Co. No. IX, p. 51; R.A.I., p. 241; L.I., p. 54; K. 54. Dt. Pref Ven (Ba Phnom).
Refers to the restoration (?) of a Śiva-*liṅga* by Ācārya Vidyāvinaya and also erection of two *liṅgas*,—Refers to Jayavarman in V. 7-B, which is evidently a later addition.

No. 23. Phnom Bayan Ins. of Bhavavarman II.
Ed. C. 252; K. 483.
Very fragmentary.—Donation to Utpanneśvara. Mentions Kongavarman.

No. 24. Phnom Penh Stele Ins. of Bhavavarman II, D. 561.
Ed. B. IV, p. 691. R.B.I., p. 161; XV (2), p. 26. L.I., p. 82; K. 79.
Probably belonged originally to the Dv. of Takeo and is now at Ecole Française—Installation of Devīcaturbhujā by the king, and donations.

No. 25. Tuol Kok Prah Stele Ins. of king Jayavarman I, D. 579.
Ed. B. XVIII (10), p. 15; K. 493;
Loc. Paddyfield, east of Tuol Kok Prah, Kompong Rursei, Dt. Prei Ven.
Foundation of the temple of God Amrātakeśvara by Jñānacandra, minister of Jayavarman I, in 579.

No. 26. Vat Prei Var Stele Ins. of king Jayavarman I, D. 587.
Ed. Co. No. X, p. 60, R.A.I., p. 248; L.I. p. 51; K. 49; Dv. Prei Ven.
Donation by king Jayavarman I to two Buddhist monks.

No. 27. Kdei Aṅ (Ang Chumnik) Stele Ins. of king Jayavarman I D. 589 (past)=667 A.D. (C. 12).
Ed. Co. No. XI, p. 64; A.I., p. 243; L.I. p. 54; K. 53; Dv. Prei Ven.
Installation of a *liṅga* and the endowment of a temple dedicated to Śiva Vijayeśvara in the town of Āḍhyapura by Siṁhadatta, physician and hereditary governor--Refers to kings Rudravarman, Bhavav°, Mahendrav° and Īśānav°—Four generations of donors, one of whom was sent on an embassy to Champā, another, a poet and a minister.

No. 28. Vat Prei Var Stone Slab Ins.; D. 589 (past).
Ed. Co. No. XII, p. 73; A.I., p. 51; K. 50; Dv. Prei Ven.
Installation of a *liṅga* of Viṣṇu-Īśa (Harihara?)

No. 29. Vat Kirivon Stone Ins. D. 592.
R.B. XXX, pp. 526, 583. K. 666; Dt. Tralac.
Installation of a liṅga.

No. 30. Tuol Prah That Pillar Ins. of Jayavarman I, D. 595.
Ed. C. 12; K. 762.
Loc. Khand of Kañcriec.
Installation of a linga (Kedāreśvara) by Rājasabhādhipati.

No. 30A. Prah Kuha Luon Ins. of Jayavarman, D. 596; R.C. 13.

No. 31. Vat Baray Stele Ins. D. 598.
Ed. Co. No. XIII, p. 75; K. 140; Dv. Baray (Kampong Savay).
Installation of an image of Śambhu—Ref. to Śaṅkara-Nārāyaṇa (?)

No. 32. Tan Kran Stele Ins. of Jayavarman I.

Invocation to Pingaleśa—genealogy of a family of royal officials (designations of various offices)—Eulogy of the king—Refers to Kāñchipura—Governor of Dhruvapura (full of dense forest) inhabited by savages (V. XIV), —Refers to Śreṣṭhapura.

No. 33. Vat Phu Stele Ins. of Jayavarman I.
Ed. B. II, p. 235; K. 367; Dt. Bassak, Laos.

No. 34. Sambor Ins. of Jayavarman I.
R.A.I., p. 306; K. 131; Dt. Krace.

No. 35. Snay Pol Stele Ins. (6th Cent. Ś).
Ed. B. XV (2), p. 21; K. 66.
Records gifts to Bhagavatī by Śālgrāmasvāmī and Āditya Svāmī (figures of Śālagrāma and sun, after the names of donors).

No. 36. Prasat Prah That Ins. (6th Cent. S').
Ed. B. XI, p. 393; K. 109; Dt. Thbon Khmum
Gift of a Ms. (*pustaka*) of Sambhava (Sambhava-parvam of Mahābhārata).

No. 37. Vat Thlen Stele Ins. (6th Cent. Ś).
R.A.I., p. 146; L. III. p. 479; K. 1. Dt. Chaudoc.
Donations of the Governors of Jeṣṭhapura and Bhavapura to God Śaṅkaranārāyaṇa.

No. 38. Prasat Pram Loveṅ Stele Ins. (6th Cent. Ś).
R.A.I., p. 139; L. III. p. 478; K. 6. Dt. Sadec (Cochin-China).
Records pious works by a priest Śrī Puṣpavaṭasvāmī, donations to God Mūlasthāna by a high official. Śucidata,—Yayamāna Vraḥ Kamratan (high dignitary) Śrī Puṣkarākṣa (the ancestor of Yaśovarman (?).

No. 39. Prasat Pram Loveṅ Stele Ins. (6th Cent. Ś).
R.A.I., p. 140; L. III. p. 478; K. 8. Dt. Sadec.
Pious donations by a chief Kṛṣṇadatta to god Śrī Amrātakeśvara.

No. 40. Camnom Stele Ins. (6th Cent. Ś).
R.A.I., pp. 195-96; *JA*. 1883 (1), p. 450. L.I., p. 16. K. 30. Dt. Prei Krabas.
Installation of god Yajñapatiśvara (Harihara ?) by Kṛṣṇamūrti; construction of temple and donations by his relations.

No. 41. Nan Khmau Stele Ins. (6th Cent. Ś).
R.A.I., p. 183; L.I., p. 31. K. 37; Dt. Bati.
—Donations to god Vrah Yama.

No. 42. Vat Tnot Stele Ins. (6th Cent. Ś).
R.A.I., p. 182 *JA*., 1883 (1), p. 449, L.I., p. 32. K. 38. Dt. Bati.
Donations to gods Śrī Gaṇapati, Vrah Svayambhū (Brahmā)—Refers to Vikramapura (old town near Bati)—mentions Jayavarman (king Jayavarman I ?).

No. 43. Vat Pret Sva Stele Ins. (6th Cent. Ś).
R.A.I., p. 182. L.I. p. 45. K. 41. Dt. Bati.
Donations to god Piṅgaleśvara (Śiva ?).

No. 44. Phnom Ngouk Stele Ins. (6th Cent. Ś).
R.A.I., p. 154. L.I., p. 49. K. 46. Dt. Kampot.
Donations to god Utpanneśvara (Utpaleśvara ? Śiva ?).

No. 45. Sambor Ins. (6th Cent. Ś).
R.B. IV, p. 742, f.n. K. 133. Dt. Kraceh.
Donations of a high official called Mahā-nauvāhaka.

No. 46. Ba Dom Stele Ins. (6th cent. Ś).
R.B. III, p. 369, L. II, p. 64. K. 360. Dt. Stun Tren (Laos).
Construction of a brick temple of Śiva and a *bhaktaśāla* and a *śilāvandhana*.

No. 47. Vihar Thom Triśūla Ins.
Ed. B. XX, pp. 6-7. K. 520. Dt. Kompon Sien.
Records that a tooth of an octogenerian was deposited under a Triśula erected by him.

No. 48. Prah That Kvan Pir Pillar Ins. D. 638.
Ed. B. IV, p. 675; R.L.I., p. 185. K. 121. Dt. Kraceh.
Installation of god Puṣkareśa by Puṣkara. As suggested by Pelliot (B. IV. p. 214) this Puṣakara may be identified with Puṣkarākṣa, prince of Aninditapura and king of Śambhupura (Co. p. 356-7).

No. 49. Lobok Srot Pillar Ins. of Jayavarman, D. 703.
Ed. B.V., p. 419. R.B. XXVIII, p. 119, K. 134. Dt. Kraceh.
The king is referred to as Brahma-kṣatra-vaṁśa
Vaiṣṇava foundations.

No. 50. Vat Tasar Moroy Stele Ins. D. 725.
R.A.I., p. 305; L.I., p. 187. K. 124. Dt. Kraceh.
Donation of the queen Jyesṭhāryâ to Śiva—mentions Jayendra, queen Nṛpendradevī and the king (who has gone to) Śrīndraloka—Donation (probably of the same queen) to God Śrimadāmrataka.

No. 51. Prasat Prei Kmen Ins. D. 782.
R.B. XXXIII, p. 1137.
Refers to Jayavarman III.

No. 52. Prasat Kok Po Ins. of Jayavarman III.
R.A.I., p. 384. K. 256. Dt. Siem Rap.
Donations by king Viṣṇuloka to god Puṇḍarikākṣa Śvetadvīpa.

No. 53. Prasat Cak (Angkor) Ins. of Jayavarman III. D. 791.
Ed. B. XXVIII, p. 115, K. 521.
The 16th regnal year of the king—Installation of Śaka Brāhmaṇa.

No. 54. Prah Ko Stele Ins. of Indravarman, D. 801.
Ed. C. p. 19. K. 713. Dt. Siem Rap
Indravarman became king in 799, Ś.—Instals three images in 801. Nos. 54-57 and 59 are nearly identical, cf. C. 17.

No. 55. Bakong Door Pillar Ins. of Indravarman, D. 801(?).
R.Co. No. XXXVII. p. 310. K. 304-306.
Five copies of the inscription.

No. 56. Bako Stele Ins. of Indravarman. D. 801.
Ed. Co. No. XXXVI. p. 297. K. 310-13. also 315-22 (of the same purport). (six copies). Dt. Siem Rap.
Genealogy of the king and his donations.

No. 57. Bakong Stele Ins. of Indravarman, D. 803.
Ed. C. 31. K. 826. Dt. Sutnikom.
Foundation of Liṅga Indreśvara—first 22 stanzas identical with Prah Ko (No. 54).

No. 58. Prasat Kandol Dom Door Pillar Ins. of Indravarman, D. 801.
Ed. C. 37. K. 809.
Mentions Indravarman and his guru Śivasoma who learnt Śāstras from Śaṅkarācārya.

No. 59. Bayang Stele Ins. of Indravarman I.
Ed. Co. No. XXXVIII, p. 312. K. 14. Dt. Tran
Foundation of a temple and two monasteries by the king at Śivapura.

No. 60. Prah Bat Stele Ins. of Yaśovarman, D. 811.
Ed. Co. No. XLIV, p. 355. K. 95. Dt. Con Prei.
Genealogy of the king—Regulations of the monasteries—Pious foundations and eulogy of the king.
There are ten replicas of this inscription (cf. Co. Nos. XLV—LIV. pp. 376-390) which contain identical verses except one which refers to the particular divinity for whom the Ins. is meant.

No. 61. Loley Stele Ins. of Yaśovarman.
Ed. Co. No. LV. p. 391.
Royal genealogy as in No. 60, but the eulogy is different.

No. 62. (A-F), Six Thnal Baray Stele Ins. of Yaśovarman.
Ed. Co. Nos. LVI-LX, pp. 420-525; B. XXXII, p. 85
62A=Co. LVI; 62 B=Co. LVII; 62C=Co. LVIII; 62D=Co. LIX; 62E=Co. LX. 62F. Ed. B. XXXII, p. 85.
These six inss. are nearly identical.

No. 63 Prasat Komnap Ins. of Yaśovarman.
Ed. B. XXXII. 88. K. 701.
Mostly identical with 62A. Genealogy identical with 61.
Regulations of a Vishṇuite Āśrama.

No. 63A. Tep Pranam Ins. of Yaśovarman.
Ed. *JA.*, 1908 (1), p. 203 1908 (2), p. 253. K. 290.
Nearly identical with Nos. 62A and 63.

No. 64. Bako Door Pillar Ins. D. 813.
R.A. II. p. 444. K. 314. Dt. Siem Rap.
Donations of Īśvaravarman to Īśvarāśrama.

No. 65. Prah Ko Stele Ins. of Yaśovarman. D. 815.
Ed. C. 28. K. 713. (See No. 54).
Donation of Yaśovarman to Parameśvara.

No. 66. Loley Door Pillar Ins. of Yaśovarman, D. 815.
Ed. Co. XXXIX-XLII (pp. 324-331). K. 324; 327; 330; 331.

No. 67. Phnom Prah Vihāra Pillar Ins. D. 815
Ed. Co. LXI, p. 525; K. 382. Dt. Mlu Prei.
Mentions king Jayavarman II with 724 as the date of accession and eulogises Śivaśakti.

No. 68. Phnom Dei Door Pillar Ins. of Yaśovarman. D. 815(?).
Ed. B. XVIII (9), p. 13.
Temple on the summit of Śrī-Purandara-parvata dedicated to Harihara.

No. 69. Phnom Sandak Stele Ins. of Yaśovarman, D. 817.
Ed. Co. XLIII, p. 331. K. 190.
Eulogy of the king and previous kings, particularly Jayavarman II.
Foundations of Somaśiva, *adhyāpaka*, nominated by the king.
The same date is given in Prasat Prei Kemen Ins. B. XXXIII, p. 1137.

No. 70. Phimanakas Door Pillar Ins. of Yaśovarman, D. 832.
Ed. Co. No. LXII, p. 545. K. 291.
Loc. Angkor Thom.
Construction of a temple of Viṣṇu—Records the date of king's death (?)

Nos. 71-72. Two Angkor Thom Inss. of Yaśovarman.
Ed. B. XXV, pp. 305-9. K. 491, 576.
Donations by the king's uncle Śrī Samaravikrama.

No. 73. Phnom Bayan Ins. of Yaśovarman.
Ed. C. 256. K. 853.
Eulogy of Amarabhāva, highly esteemeed by the king and appointed by Indravarman as chief of Indrāśrama.

No. 74. Vat Thipedi Door Pillar Ins. of Īśānavarman II. D. 832.
Ed. Melange S. Lévi, p. 213. R.A. II., p. 379. K. 253.
Dt. Siem Rap.
It contains two different Inss. A and B. A gives eulogy of Yaśovarman and his two sons, and records the erection of the temple, in 832, by Śikhāśiva.—Marginal Text in Khmer records some donations of another person in 834. B. refers to Sūryavarman and commemorates the restoration, in 927, of a *liṅga*, consecrated 95 years ago Śikhāsiva, predecessor of a certain Kṛtīndrapaṇḍita of whom it gives the genealogy, giving a new instance of succession, in female line, of *hotars* of different kings. (The date 832 may not belong to the reign of Īśānavarman II. Cf. *JGIS*. III, p. 65).

No. 75. Vihar Kuk (Vat Cakret) Stele Ins. of Harṣavarman I. D. 834 (?).
Ed. Co. No. LXIII, p. 551. R. *JGIS*. III, p. 65. K. 61. Dt. Prei Ven.
Donation of the king to Adrivyādhapureśa (Śiva).

No. 76. Prasat Thom (Koh Ker) Ins. of Jayavarman IV. D. 843.
Ed. B. XXXI, p. 13. Co. No. LXIV, p. 555. K. 682.

No. 77. Two Koh Ker Inss. D. 843.
Ed. B. XXXI, p. 15. K. 682.

No. 78. Tuol Pei Ins. of Harṣavarman (?) D. 844.
Ed. B. XXXI, p. 17. R.A. I. p. 443. *JGIS*. III. p. 65. K. 164. Dt. Sron.
The name of the king is doubtful, but, if correct, it is the only Ins. datable in his reign.

No. 79. Coṅ An Pillar Ins. of Jayavarman IV. D. 844.
R.B. XXXI, p. 16; A.I. p. 292. K. 99. Dt. Thbon Khmum.
Order of the king to Pṛthivīndravarman—Installation of gods Tribhuvanaikanātha and Campeśvara (Kṛṣṇa ?) and donations.

No. 80. Prasat Neang Khmau Ins. of Jayavarman IV. D. 850.
R.A. I, p. 183. K. 35. Dt. Bati.
It gives the year 850 as the date of the accession of the king.

No. 81. Koh Ker Pillar Ins. of Jayavarman IV. D. 851 (?), 852, 854.
Ed. Co. No. LXIV, p. 555. K. 184, 186, 187, 188.

No. 82. Prasat Andon Ins. of Jayavarman IV.
Ed. C. 61, K. 675.

No. 83. Prasat Damrei Ins. of Jayavarman IV.
Ed. C. 56. K. 677.

No. 83A. Prasat Kok (wrongly described as Prasat Preah Dak) Ins. of Jayavarman IV.
R.A. II. p. 419. K. 339. Dt. Siem Rap.
Invocation of the three Buddhist *Ratnas*—genealogy of the king from Jayavarman II—Conquest of Champā by Jayavarman IV.

No. 84. Phnom Bayan Ins. of Harṣavarman II. D. 863.
Ed. C. 260. K. 854. Dt. Tonlap.
Invocation to Utpannakeśvara followed by the eulogy of Jayavarman IV who appears, from some expressions, to have usurped the throne. The date is one year earlier than that generally assumed for the accession of the king.

No. 85. Vat Kdei Car Stele Ins. of Harṣavarman II. D. 864.
R.A. I. p. 372; B. XV (2), p. 25. K. 157. Dt. Kompon Svay
Gives the date of the accession of the king.

No. 86. Trapan Samliot Stele Ins. of Rājendravarman, D. 866.
R.A. I. p. 165. K. 19. Dt. Tran.
Donations.—Year of accession.

No. 87. Two Prah Put Lo Rock Inss. D. 869.
Ed. *JA*. 1914 (1), pp. 638, 644. R.A. I, p. 426. K. 173-4.
Religious aphorisms; eulogy of their authors who were ascetics.

No. 88. Prasat Pram Door Pillar Ins. of Rājendravarman D. 869 (February, 948 A.D.).

Ed. B. XIII (6), p. 17. K. 180. Dt. Kompon Svay.
Eulogy of king Jayavarman IV and his two sons. Installation of two *liṅgas* by Rudrācārya, the teacher of the king, and a pupil of Śivasoma, the famous *guru* of Indravarman.

No. 89. Baksei Camkron Door Pillar Ins. of Rājendravarman, D. 869.
Ed. *JA.* 1909 (1), p. 467. R.A. III, p. 80. K. 286. Loc. Mt. Bakheng.
It gives the mythical story of the foundation of Kambuja by Riṣi Kambu and refers to the kings Śrutavarman, Rudravarman, Jayavarman II and his successors.

No. 89A. Mebon Ins. of Rājendravarman, D. 874.
Ed. B. XXV, p. 309. Loc. Near Angkor Thom.
Genealogy and eulogy of Rājendravarman.

No. 90. Thvar Kdei Ins. of Rājendravarman. D. 874 (or 871) and 879.
R.A. I, p. 444. K. 165. Dt. Sron.
Queen Mahendradevī informs king Rājendravarman of the territories enjoyed by her ancestors in Dvāravatī, Sahakāra, and other lands.—Donations to Campeśvara. Invocation to Viṣṇu, called Vāsudeva, Hari, Nārāyaṇa, and Madhvari, identified with Oṁ.

No. 91. Phnom Sandak Stele Ins. D. 878.
R.A. I, p. 393. K. 102. Dt. Cikren.
Royal donations to Śivapura (Phnom Sandak).

No. 92. Bat Cum Ins. of Rājendravarman, D. 882.
Ed. *JA*. 1908 (2), p. 213. R.A. III, p. 11. K. 266-8. Dt. Siem Rap.
Eulogy of Rājendravarman who embellished Yaśodharapurī, deserted for a long time, and destroyed Champā and other foreign kingdoms.
Mahāyāna Buddhist Divinities—Eulogy of the Buddhist minister Kavīndrārimthana and his pious foundations.

No. 93. Pre Rup Stele Ins. of Rājendravarman, D. 883.
Ed. C. 73. K. 806. Dt. Siem Rap.
Genealogy of the king.—Conquest of Champā by the king.

No. 94. Phnom Trap Ins. D. 875, 882, 884.
R.A. I. p. 322. K. 94. Dt. Con Prei.
Installation of the images of Aja (882) and of Upendra (884). Arrival of Bhadrayogīśvara in 875.

No. 95. Neak Ta Carek Ins. D. 884.
R.A. I, p. 384. K. 181. Dt. Cikren.
Judgment of the king against Vīrabhaktigarjita, chief of Vīrapura, who had removed the boundary and reaped the corn of a field which was granted to another person. The chief was fined 10 ounces of gold. His younger brother, who ordered the reaping of corn, and another who instigated the crime were given 103 stripes on their books.

No. 96. Don Tri Ins. of Rājendravarman, D. 888.
R.A. II, p. 283. K. 198. Dt. Battambang.
Royal order to a number of officers whose names and offices are given—Buddhist divinities Parameśvarārya-maitrideva.

No. 97. Bantay Srei Ins. of Jayavarman V. D. 890
Ed. C. 147. K. 842.
(Almost a replica of K. 619, B. XXVIII. p. 46 and of K. 662. B. XXIX, p. 292).
Foundation of the temple by Yajñavarāha, the *guru* of the king Eulogy of Rājendravarman who conquered Champā—Eulogy of the king.

No. 98. Tuol Kul Ins. D. 890.
R. *JGIS*, III, 65, B. XXXV, p. 493. K. 831. Dt. Mon.
Refers to an address presented to Īśānavarman II in 847 Śāka, the only known date of this king and evidence that he actually ascended the throne.

No. 99. Angkor Vat Ins. of Jayavarman V. D. 890. K. 579.
Phnom Bakhen Ins. of Jayavarman V. D. 890. K. 464.
Identical in some parts.
Ed. B. XXV, p. 363. B. XI, p. 396.
Gives the date 890 as the commencement of his reign.

No. 100. Bantay Srei Ins. of Jayavarman V. D. 891.
Ed. C. 144. K. 570.
Foundation of the king to Tribhuvanamaheśvara (i.e. Bantay Srei).

No. 101. Bantay Srei Ins. D. 891.
Ed. Memoires Arch. EFEO Nos. 2, 74. K. 571.

No. 102. Kok Svay Prahm Ins. D. 891.
Ed. C. 187. K. 848. Dt. Sutnikom.
Royal order to the *grāmavṛddha* and *puruṣapradhāna* of Hariharālaya. It proves that Svay Prahm which forms part of the Roluos group was situated in the territory of Harihanālaya. This confirms the view of Coedes (B. XXVIII, p. 121) that Roluos represents Hariharālaya where Jayavarman II lived twice and died, and which was the capital of his successors till Yaśovarman I founded Yaśodharapura on the site of Angkor.

No. 103. Prah Einkosi Ins. of Rājendravarman D. 890 and Jayavarman V., D. 892.
Ed. Co. No. XIV, p. 77; C. 160. K. 262, 263 (K. 668—Replica). Dt. Siem Rap.
A—Refers to Rājendravarman's predecessor, a king of the race of Kauṇḍinya who lived in Aninditapura.
B—Eulogy of Jayavarman and the diverse foundations of his younger sister Indralakṣmī and her husband, the Brāhmana Divākarabhaṭṭa, a native of the bank of the Yamunā (in India).

No. 104. Kok Rosi Ins. of Jayavarman V. D. 891.
Ed. B. XXVIII, pp. 113-14.

No. 105. Basak Stele Ins. of Rājendravarman.
Ed. B. XV (2), p. 22. K. 70. Dt. Romduol.
Donation of a chief named Nṛpendrāyudha, *pārśvadhara* of the king to god Vakakākēśvara—Refers to the installation by the king of five images at Angkor on the island of Mebon in the centre of Thnal Baray (Eastern) (Yaśodhara-taṭāka).

No. 106. Basak Stele Ins.
R.B. XV (2), p. 20. K. 71.
Religious foundation by Rājakula Mahāmantrī (minister of Rājendravarman).

No. 107. Srey Santhor Ins. of Jayavarman V.
Ed. *Revue Archeologique*, 1883, pp. 182-192.

No. 108. Prasat Komphus Ins. of Jayavarman V. D. 894.
Ed. C. 159. K. 669.
It is almost a replica of No. 103.

No. 109. Prasat Nak Buos Ins. of Jayavarman V. D. 896.
R. Co. 381. K. 343.
Royal gift to Śivapada.

No. 110. Phnom Bantay Nan Ins. D. 902, 903.
R.A. II, p. 306 (with commentaries of Kern). K. 214.
No. 5 above refers to it as Śaiva temple under Bhavavarman—but this inscription refers to Mahāyāna Buddhist divinities, on which Kern has commented

No. 111. Prah Einkosi Inss. D. 883, 890, 902, 904, 906.
R.A. II, pp. 407-410. (cf. No. 103 above).
Foundation in favour of a monastery called Vidyāśrama (883 Ś), Temple of Dwijendrapura (890). Divākarabhaṭṭa, priest of this temple, receives donations (902) which are confirmed (904) and added to (906). Dwijendrapura (Temple of Prah Einkosi) inherits parts of the slaves of Vidyāśrama.

No. 112. Prasat Car Ins. of Jayavarman V. D. 901, 916.
R.A. II, p. 387. K. 257. Dt. Siem Raj
Installation of various Brahmanical divinities and donations to them by Narapativīravarman.

No. 113. Prasat Trapan Coṅ Ins.
Ed. B. XXIX, p. 292. Fragmentary; almost identical with No. 114.

No. 114. Prasat Sek Ta Tuy Ins. of Jayavarman V.
Ed. B. XXVIII, p. 46. R.B. XXIX. p. 291. f.n.l. K. 617. Dt. Cikren.
Jayavarman s victory in Champā. Reference to Śrīparvata in the Dakṣiṇāpatha—Religious acts and donations of the royal *guru* Yajñavarāha.

No. 115. Angkor Thom Ins. 9th Cent.
Ed. B. XXIX, p. 343. *JA*. Vol. CCXX (1932) p. 50. K. 643.
Invocations to various forms of Viṣṇu and other gods.

No. 116. Pon Pra Thvar Grotto Ins 9th or 10th Cent.
Ed. B. XI. 398. K. 172.
Interesting account of a cave.

No. 117. Prasat Khna Ins. of Udayādityavarman D. 902, 923.
Ed. B. XI, p. 400. K. 356. Dt. Mlu Prei.
It definitely proves the existence of the king and gives his date and genealogy showing his relationship with king Jayavarman V.

No. 118. Prasam Thom Ins. of Udayādityavarman D. 923.
Ed. C. 50. K. 682. Loc. Koh ker.
Royal order about donations to Pṛthivīnarendra and Vīrendrārimathana.

No. 119. Prasat Ak Yom Ins. D. 923.
R.B. XXXIII, p. 531. K. 752. Dt. Puok
It proves that the 'Western Baray' beneath which the stone was interred, was excavated after 923.

No. 120. Sambor Ins. D. 923.
Ed. B. XXVIII, p. 142. R.A. I, p. 307. K. 125. Dt. Kraceh.
It definitely locates Śambhu-pura, famous since the sixth century. It may refer to Udayādityavarman I or Sūryavarman.

No. 121. Stun Crap Ins. of Jayavīravarmadeva D. 925.
R.B. XXXIV, p. 423, B. XXXI, p. 620. K. 693. Dt. Battambang.
Application of Brahmaputra claiming a foundation made by his ancestor Paṇḍitāṅkura Ācārya Dharmādhipati before the time of Yśovarman. The judgment of the king in favour of the claimant—There is an image of Yama (Dharmādhipati).

No. 122. Tuol Prasat Ins. of Jayavīravarman D. 925.
R.A. I, pp. 379-381. B. XXXIV, p. 423; K. 158. Dt. Kampon Svay.
Gives the date 924 for Jayavarman and 925 for Jayavīravarman living in Jayendranagarī—Refers to donations made by many previous kings.

No. 123. Prasat Kok Po Inscription of Jayavarman D. 900, 906, (also dates 901, 926).
Ed. B. XXXVII, p. 379. K. 255, 256, 814.

No. 124. Prah Ko Ins. of Jayavīravarman D. 927.
Ed. C. 189. K. 717. Dt. Sutnikom.
Śikhāśiva's grandson Vinaya, a Professor, obtained favour from the king.—It proves that Jayavīravarman was different from Sūryavarman—gives the date of accession of Jayavarman IV (850) and Rājendravarman (866).

No. 125. Prasat Dambauk Khpos Ins. of Jayavīravarman D. 927.
R.A. I., p. 420; B. XXXIV, p. 423. K. 196.

No. 126. Roban Romas Ins. of Sūryavarman I. D. 923.
R.B. XXXIV, p. 422. K. 153. Dt. Kompon Svay.
Donation of Someśvara Paṇḍita.

No. 127. Prasat Tapan Run Ins. D. 924 (or 934).
R.B. XXXIV, p. 422. K. 705. Dt. Kompon Svay.

No. 128. Prah Nan Ins. of Sūryavarman I. D. 924.
R.A. I, p. 328. K. 89.
The king founded Bhadreśvarāśrama for the gods Liṅgapura and Liṅgaśodhana. It was consecrated by Śrī Prathivīndra Paṇḍita of the country of Ramani—Donations to *ācāryas* living in the monastery—Refers to the hereditary governor of Bhavapura—deified statue of Jayavarman II—god Jalaṅgeśvara.

No. 129. Tuol Don Srei Ins. of Sūryavarman I. D. 924.
R.B. XXXIV, p. 427; XXXV, p. 493. K. 834. Dt. Baray, Kompon Thom.
Refers to a war of 9 years by Sūryavarman who became king in 924. Gives the history of a family of royal officials since the reign of Jayavarman II.

No. 130. Tep Pranam Ins. of Sūryavarman I. D. 927.
R.A. III, p. 112. K. 290.

No. 131. Vat Phu Ins. of Sūryavarman I. D. 928
R.B. XXXIII (531). K. 720. Dt. Bassac.

No. 132. Prasat Trapan Ins. of Jayavīravarman D. 928.
Ed. B. XXVIII, p. 58. K. 598. Dt. Sutnikom.
Donation to a temple (Vaiṣnava) of land in Aninditapura—genealogy of Pañcagavya or Kavīndra-paṇḍita who founded the temple and whose ancestors served the kings from Jayavarman II—It fixes the location of Aninditapura (p. 61).

No. 133. Phnom Prah Net Prah Ins. of Jayavīravarman D. 927-29.
R.A. II, p. 322. B. XXXIV, p. 423. K. 216. Dt. Battambang.
Order of the king (927)—foundations at Śivapada or Śaivapada (928); a royal order (king not named) in 929.

No. 134. Phnom Sanke Kon Ins. of Sūryavarman I. D. 928, 929,
R.A. II, p. 246. B. XXXIV, p. 424. K. 232. Dt. Krabin (Siam).
Royal order about a donation.

No. 136. Phimanaka Inscriptions of Sūryavarman I, D. 933.
R.A. II, p. 233. K. 342. Dt. Mlu Prei.
Royal donations.

No. 136. Phimanaka Inscriptions of Sūryavarman I, D. 933.
Ed. B. XIII (6), p. 11. K. 292. Loc. Angkor Thom.
Eight Inss. on the pillars of Gopura leading to the interior of the royal palace at Angkor Thom, reproducing, in identical terms, the formula of oath pronounced by certain officials of the court of the king.
Two other replicas of the same.
R.B. XIII (6), p. 12.

No. 137. Inscriptions of Bantay Srei D. 933.
Ed. Memoir Arch. EFEO, I. Nos. 3, 4, p. 77. K. 569, 572.
For other Ins. K. 573-575, of *Ibid*, Nos. 8, 7, 6,

No. 138. Phnom Cisor Ins. of Sūryavarman I. D. 937, 939, 941.
R.A. I, pp. 191-92. K. 33, 31. Dt. Bati.
Foundation of monasteries called Yogendrālaya and Yogendrapura—god Vṛddheśvara.

No. 139. Lopburi (Siam) Ins. of Sūryavarman I. D. 944, 947.
R.A. II, p. 81. K. 410.
Royal regulations—Religious institutions must offer to the king merits of their austerity—those disturbing them to be punished.

No. 140. Prasat Ben Ins. of Sūryavarman I D. 948.
R.A. II, pp. 351-52. K. 230. Dt. Sisophon.
Royal orders.

No. 141. Vat Ek. Ins. D. 949.
R.A. II, p. 301. K. 211. Dt. Battambang.
Donations of Yogīśvarapaṇḍita of Vyādhapura

No. 142. Ta Nen Ins. of Sūryavarman I D. 949.
R.A. II, p. 302. K. 212. Dt. Battambang.
Royal order to Śrī Gaurīśvarapaṇḍita of the country of Śivagupta concerning four *āśramas* (named Yogīśvar-ālaya, °āvāsa etc.).

No. 143. Prasat Sek Ta Tuy Ins. of Sūryavarman I, D. 961.
Ed. B. XXVIII, p. 56. K. 618. Dt. Cikren.

No. 144. Prasat Khna Ins. of Sūryavarman I. D. 963.
Ed. C. 195. K. 660. Dt. Mul Prei.
Donation to Śakabrāhmana, by brother of the queen Vīra-Lakṣmī.

No. 145. Four Baset Inss. D. 958, 964.
R.A. II, pp. 294-95. K. 205-207. Dt. Battambang.
Donation to Jayakṣetra by Guṇapativarman.

No. 146. Phnom Pra Vihar Ins. of Sūryavarman I. D. 948, 949, 960, 963, 969.
R.A. II, pp. 208-9. Co. p. 527. K. 380, 381, 382.
God Śrī Śikhareśvara and Śrī Vṛddheśvara.

No. 147. Phnom Sandak Ins. of Sūryavarman I. D. 963, 971.
R.A. I, p. 394. K. 195. Dt. Cikren.
Royal orders.

No. 148. Prasat Kev. Ins. of Sūryavarman I.
Ed. Co. No. XV, p. 97. K. 275-278. Dt. Siem Rap.
Eulogy of the king and donations of Śivācārya, descendant of Jayavarman II (?)

No. 149. Prah Khan Ins. of Sūryavarman I.
Ed. B. IV, p. 672. K. 161. Dt. Kompon Svay.
Gives 924 as the date of accession of the king who was versed in different *śāstras*,

No. 150. Prasat Roluh (Sisophon) Ins. of Udayādityavarman II. D. 971. 972.
R.A. II, p. 326-7. K. 219.
The king ascended the throne in 971. In 972 granted in perpetuity the country of Stuk Rman (the family of its possessors having all died) to Śrī Jayendrapaṇḍita.

No. 151. Sdok Kak Thom Ins. of Udayādityavarman II, D. 974.
Ed. B. XV (2), p. 53. K. 235. Dt. Krabin (Siam).
The foundations of a family whose members (through mothers) were hereditary royal priests and great priests of Devarāja from the time of Jayavarman II to that of Sūryavarman I.

No. 152. Phun Da (Kompon Chnan) Ins. D. 976.
Ed. *JA*. 1882 (1), p. 208. R.A. I, p. 362. K. 139.
Installation of a Śivaliṅga by an ascetic, named Jñānapriya Āryamaitrin—Mystic philosophy of the Upanishads.

No. 153. Prah Nok Ins. D. 988.
Ed. Co. No. XVIII, p. 140. K. 289. Dt. Siem Rap.
Records the victory and pious foundations of Senāpati Saṅgrāma (details of his various campaigns)—genealogy of the donor containing names of various kings served by his ancestors.

No. 154. Prasat Prah Khset (Siem Rap) Ins. of Udayārkavarman D. 988, 989.
Ed. Co. No. XIX, p. 173. K. 237.
Restoration of a liṅga by Saṁkarsha, son of the king's sister, in 988, to which was added in 989 the images of Brahmā, Viṣṇu and Buddha—the previous history of the *liṅga* (given by Sūryavarman, broken by Kambu in course of a fight mentioned in No. 153).

No. 154A. Prasat Khna Ins. of Udayādityavarman II, D. 982.
Ed. C. 198. K. 661. Dt. Mul Prei.
Royal donation to golden Lakṣmī—Eulogy of Sūryavarman—Refers to Jayendra-Paṇḍita and Kavīndra-Paṇḍita.

No. 155. Palhal (Battambang) Ins. of Harsavarman III. D. 991.
Ed. B. XIII (6), p. 27. K. 449.
Installation of Tribhuvaneśvara by two persons whose genealogy is given in detail. Perhaps they belonged to the family of Saṅgrāma mentioned in No. 153.—The members of this Brāhmaṇa family were elephant driver, concubine of the king, artisans and priests.—It shows that the Brāhmaṇas of Kambuja did not scrupulously follow the rules of caste.

No. 156. Prasat Sralau Ins. of Harṣavarman III. D. 987, 993.
Ed. C. 221. K. 782. Dt. Puok.
Eulogy of Harṣavarman who became king in 987—Restoration of a town founded by Jayavarman and abandoned by Udayādityavarman—mentions Sūryavarman's queen—Installation of *liṅga* and images of Viṣṇu and Śiva.

No. 157. San Sung Ins. 10th Cent.
Ed. *Recueil des inscriptions du Siam* (Coedès) II. No. 20, 25.
Loc. Lopburi (Siam).

No. 158. Loṅvek Ins. of Harṣavarman III.
Ed. Co. XVII, p. 122. K. 136. Dt. Loṅvek.
Donations by the members of a family, called Saptadevakula; one of them Śaṅkarapaṇḍita was the priest of three kings Sūryavarman, Udayādityavarman and Harṣavarman.

No. 159. Samror Ins. of Harṣavarman III. D. 1011.
R.B. XXIX, p. 299; A. II, p. 391.

No. 160. Nom Van Ins. of Jayavarman VI. D. 1004.
R.B. XXIX, p. 298-9. A. II, p. 111.

No. 161. Prasat Kok Po Ins. of Jayavarman VI, D. 1018.
Ed. B. XXXVII, p. 413. K. 814. Dt. Puok.
Royal donation.

No. 162. Phnon Bayan Ins. of Dharaṇīdravarman I. D. 1029.
Ed. C. 267. K. 852. Dt. Tonlap.
Installation by the king of the god of Bhadreśvarāśrama—An unpublished Ins. from Phnom Sandak (K. 191) shows that 1029 Śaka was the date of king's accession (C. 267).

No. 163. Prasat Trau Ins. of Dharaṇīndravarman I. D. 1031.
R.A. II, p. 377. K. 249. Dt. Siem Rap.
Religious foundation of a private family.

No. 164. Phimai Ins. Dated 1031, 1034.
R.A. II, 122. K. 397. Loc. Rajasima (Siam).

No. 165. Vat Phu Ins. of Sūryavarman II. D. 1035, 1061.
R.B. XXIX, p. 303. K. 366.
It gives the date of accession of Sūryavarman II (1035) who united the two portions of the kingdom.

No. 166. Phnom Cisor Ins. of Sūryavarman II. D. 1038.
R.A. I, p. 192. K. 32. Dt. Bati.
Donation by an ascetic to god of Sūryaparvata.

No. 167. Phnom Sandak Ins. of Sūryavarman II. D 1041.
R.A. I, p. 395. K. 194. Dt. Cikren.
Genealogy of a royal priestly family; mentions Jayavarman V, Udayādityavarman (acc. 971), and the next three kings who were consecrated by Divākarapaṇḍita—Sūryavarman's relation with his predecessors—Accomplishments of the young king—performance of koṭihoma etc., by Divākarapaṇḍita.

No. 168. Phnom Pra Vihar Ins. of Sūryavarman II, D. 1040, 1041, 1043.
R.A. II, p. 213. K. 383. Dt. Mlu Prei.
—The substance is nearly the same as that of the preceding one No. 167. viz., details of Divākarapaṇḍita.

No. 169. Trapan Don On Ins. of Sūryavarman II D. 1048.
R.A. II, p. 380. K. 254. Dt. Siem Rap.

It gives the posthumous names of 3 kings; Haraṣavarman II—Sadāśivapada, Jayavarman VI—Paramakaivalyapada, Dharaṇīndravarman I—Paramanishkalapada.
Various religious donations to god of Liṅgapura.—Refers to Divākarapaṇḍita.

No. 170. Vat Phu (Bassak) Ins. D. 1058.
Ed. B. XV (2), p. 107. K. 475.
Donations of Mūlasūtra and his father, of the country of Bhadreśvarāspada, of the Corporation of workers of Śreṣṭhapura *viṣaya*, to the god of Liṅgapura, called Liṅgapurāśrama.—various donations to the temple of Vat Phu dated 1024, 1026, 1034, 1044, 1049, and 1061 are mentioned in another Ins. K. 366 (A. II. p. 163). The temple was dedicated to Bhadreśvara (Śiva), though reference is also made to the installation of Viṣṇu.

No. 171. Ban That (Bassac) Ins. of Sūryavarman II.
Ed. B. XII (2). K. 364.
Long eulogy of kings Jayavarman VI, Dharaṇīdravarman I and Sūryavarman II by a *muni* who was hereditary priest of the *liṅga* installed on mount Bhadreśvara.

No. 172. Phnom Run. Ins. of Sūryavarman II.
R.B. XXIX, p. 300. K. 384.

No. 173. Prasat Cikren Ins.
Ed. B. XV (2). pp. 19-20. K. 417. Dt. Cikren.
Buddhist;—donation to Lokeśvara by Umā, a daughter of Saṅgrāma, of glorious exploits, and wife of Maharṣi Śri Mahīdharavarman.

Nos. 174-175. Two Phnom Svan Inss. one D. 1088.
R.B. XXIX, p. 304.

No. 176. Xaiya Buddha Image Ins. D. 1100 (?).
Ed. B. XVIII (6), p. 33. K. 504.
The date is written as 11006—Refers to Mahārāja Trailokyarājamaulibhūṣaṇavarmmadeva, and Mahāsenāpati Galānai who governed Grahi, which may be identified with Kia-lo-hi (See *Suvarnadvipa*, pp. 194-95).

No. 177. Ta Prohm Ins. of Jayavarman VII, D. 1108.
Ed. B. VI, p. 44. K. 273.
Genealogy of the king, his eulogy, and a series of religious foundations.

No. 178. Sayfong Ins. of Jayavarman VII. D. 1108.
Ed. B. III, p. 18. K. 368. Dt. Vien chang (Laos).
For its 8 or 9 replicas cf. B. III, p. 460.
Mahāyāna Buddhist invocation—Eulogy of the king who ascended the throne in 1104—Personnel and furniture of the *hospital*—Regulations.

No. 179. Prasat Tor Ins. of Jayavarman VII. D. 1111 (or 1117).
Ed. C. 227. K. 892. Dt. Sism Rap.

Bhūpendrapaṇḍita, the donor, and his family serving three preceding kings—Genealogy of the donor—Installation by the king of a golden image of his maternal grandfather Harṣavarman III—Construction of a *vihāra*, surrounded by āśrama—victory against the Chams and a king of the west.

No. 180. Angkor Thom (Prasat Crun) Ins. of Jayavarman VII.
R.B. XXVIII, p. 86; XXIX, p. 306. K. 597.
Refers to the construction of Bayon and Angkor Thom by the king—United Champā with Kambuja.

No. 181. Phimanaka Ins. of Jayavarman VII.
Ed. B. XXV, p. 372; XXIX, p. 319. K. 485.
Religious foundation of Indradevī.

No. 182. Bantay Chmar Ins. of Yaśovarman.
Ed. B. XXIX, p. 309, R.A. II, p. 344. K. 226-227.
Long description of a fight between Yaśovarman and a king of Champā named Śrī Jaya Indravarman—commemorates the heroic achievements of Śrī Śrīndrakumāra and his deification.

No. 183. Phimanaka Bilingual Ins. (12th century).
Ed. B. XVIII (9), p. 9. K. 484. Dt. Siem Rap.
Stanza praying for the preservation of the Buddhist tree (Āśvattha), identified with Brahmanical gods, against destruction and from all damages.

No. 184. Angkor Thom Ins. D. 1217 (?)
Ed. B. XXV, p. 393. K. 488.
Refers to Jayavarman, Śrī-Śrīndravarman and his queen.

No. 185. Kok Svay Chek Pali Ins. of Śrīndravarman D. 1230
Ed. B. XXXVI, p. 14. Dt. Puok.
It is the oldest Pali Ins.—It extends the known regnal period of the king by one year.

No. 186. Maṅgalārtha Temple Ins. of Śrīndrajayavarman.
Ed. B. XXV, p. 393; Loc. Angkor Thom.
It gives the list of kings who succeeded Jayavarman VII.

No. 187. Angkor Vat Ins. of Jayavarmādiparameśvara.
Ed. Co. No. LXV, p. 560. K. 300.
Royal donations—Brāhmaṇa Sarvajñamuni, who came from Āryadeśa (India).

N.B.—Three early inscriptions of Fu-nan, not included in this list, are discussed in the text, pp. 33-4, 40-42.

INDEX